There Is *More* to Life

Moving from the Finite Limits of Self to the
Immeasurable Expanse of God

Dr. Tom Kinnan

Some of the best sermons are conversations, and some of these conversations are captured in print, like in this book. Dr. Kinnan invites us into his personal narrative while addressing theological questions amidst modern challenges. "When COVID19 hit, the church came face-to-face with a startling reality. She had become so focused on gathering that she had neglected going." Now *that* will preach.

Jerry Pattengale, Ph.D., scholar, author of over 20 books, and founding scholar and senior advisor to the president at Museum of the Bible (DC)

Knowledge coupled with application brings wisdom. Tom has the ability to open up the Scriptures in such a way that God's wisdom is clear and leaves its mark on our lives. Through insight, application, and transparency, he weaves a tapestry of wisdom that drapes itself around our journey through life and helps us find some handles that give stability and enable us to move forward in life. Enter into *There Is More to Life* with expectation. You will not be disappointed.

Jim Garlow, Ph.D., CEO of Well Versed, author of 19 books

Tom Kinnan is a longtime friend. He is uniquely qualified to speak to difficult and sensitive topics in this meaningful book. The reader will immediately recognize that Tom is not writing from the sidelines but as one who has personally long-participated in life's most difficult journeys. Overflowing with wisdom, insight, and personal vulnerability, *There Is More to Life* is for everyone who desires a more honest transformational relationship with Jesus. I highly recommend [this book] for anyone seeking a deeper understanding of the expansive love of Jesus.

Jimmy Dodd, founder and CEO of PastorServe, author of *Survive or Thrive*, *Six Relationships Every Pastor Needs*, *Pastors Are People Too*, and *What Great Leaders Get Right*

The bounteous perspectives and the inspired word that Tom Kinnan gives in his book *There Is More to Life* constitute the truth of the abundant life that we are called to live. There is, in addition, great benefit to be derived from the application of the

book. This is particularly valuable for those who seek a deeper relationship with our God. The rich devotional stories and exceedingly wise observations, as well as the notes and questions, together form a perfect treasure of instructive and delightful reading. I believe that God honors the faithful and Tom's book is an act of faith. It invites people to enter a place of love and forgiveness and calls us to live a spiritual life. It is a blessing to read.
Lizet Ribeiro, host of *The JA Show* podcast (Apple Podcasts No. 1 in Self-Improvement)

How is it possible for us to comprehend a God who does the unimaginable and whose power is unmeasurable? Tom Kinnan invites us to dive into the deep end of the pool and experience for ourselves the limitless and all-encompassing nature of God. Through his own life experiences, he reminds us that God does His best and most amazing work when we are in over our heads and have the courage to trust completely and surrender all of our hopes and dreams to Him. This is a must-read for all who are ready to dive in the deeper places of the heart and experience the "immeasurably more" of God.
David J. Spittal, Ed.D., President of MidAmerica Nazarene University

With a call to action that emulates the gentle, uncompromising words of Jesus himself, Dr. Kinnan challenges us to return to the foundation of our faith so that we can experience the hope, joy, and security offered only through relationship and obedience to God. With droplets of humor and minus the fluff, the message is clear: Cultivate a relationship with God and experience a life that is immeasurably more than ever imagined. In Dr. Kinnan fashion, he has prepared an eloquently simple guide, born from scripture, and elucidated through his gift of writing.
Stephanie Wick, Ph.D., LCMFT, LCAC, owner of Andrews & Associates Counseling

Tom Kinnan catapults us into an awareness of the enormity of God, then reins us back into our childhood to set the stage for encountering the God who calls us to "more" of the life we were born to live in Jesus Christ. He gives the reader a steady diet of real-life vulnerability, mixed with profound and practical insights about ourselves and God's dreams for us, sprinkled with his funky humor. Growing in the faith and in Christlike character does not happen by magic or even by miracle. It requires a liberating submission to Christ that motivates us to make every effort to add to our faith the "more" that He has made available to us. God's desire is that our lives be practically and eternally effective and productive. This book helps us find the pathway to God's "immeasurably more" and an assurance that *There Is More to Life*.

David Holdren, pastor, teacher, author, former Wesleyan General Superintendent; husband, father, follower

In this book, Dr. Tom challenges the reader to examine their walk of faith and not settle for simply a "Sunday-morning Christianity." As an experienced pastor, Dr. Tom understands the predicament of believers who have been living out a half-hearted walk with Christ instead of embracing the God who gives immeasurably more than they could ever imagine. This immeasurably more comes in the recognition of who God is and by being conformed to the image of Christ. By drawing on the text of writings by the Apostles Paul and Peter, the reader can dive into the Scriptures with the intent of life change. With questions for reflection and space for writing, this book becomes a tool for the discipleship journey, and would fit well into a small group curriculum or for individual study.

Brenda K. Woods, M.D., FAAFP, physician, lay leader, seminary graduate

In this book, my friend Tom Kinnan, in his engaging way, encourages believers to get out of the shallows of faith, where many believers tend to dwell, and go deep with God. He explains the practical things we need to do to build on the foundation of our faith in Christ and then reminds us that these are only ways to cooperate with the Holy Spirit's divine enablement. He is the One who does the work in us and through us. I highly recommend this book to anyone, especially anyone who finds that they have grown stagnate in their growth in Christ.

Richard Emery, former Wesleyan pastor, presently transitional interim pastor at New Church Specialties

Life can sometimes overwhelm us, and we get so busy in what we are doing that we forget the importance of focusing on who we are, not just what we do. Tom compels us to go deeper in our understanding of who we are by knowing who God is. *There Is More to Life* challenges us to stop living on the surface and move into the depths of our understanding of God. When you read this book, you'll be challenged. Buckle up and prepare yourself for a journey into the expanse of God.

Leslie Washington, CEO of Blue Beacon Solutions

To my Dad and Mom, Bill and June Kinnan, who introduced me to Jesus and have continually shown me the immeasurably more offered by Christ. And to my kids, Heather and Jeff Semple and David and Katy Kinnan, who live out the immeasurably more in their lives and ministries. My love for all of them is immeasurable.

CONTENTS

The Expanse of God 3

The Foundation of Our Faith 7

The Characteristics of Faith 25

Breaking Sinful Patterns 45

Cultivating Godly Relationships 63

Going Deeper: The Practice of Submission 87

Falling into the "Whole" of God 105

Knee-Deep in a Bottomless Pit 123

How Do You Fit a Boeing 747 into Your Garage? 139

A System of "Waits" and Measures 153

It's Your Time 169

About the Author 171

About Sermon To Book 173

Notes 175

The Expanse of God

We live in a world filled with weights and measures, scales and rulers, measuring cups and odometers. We measure everything. We count, we assess, we number, and we calculate. We put boundaries and limits on people and situations. We give projects starting and stopping points. This is because when we measure things, they seem easier to control, to govern, and to replicate.

Measuring gives us some level of precision, but it can also mislead us into thinking that we are the ones who determine outcomes.

In the midst of our tightly regulated society, God has called us to live beyond what is measured and controlled. This is how Christ taught us to live.

- Jesus looked into the faces of five thousand men and their wives and children, and He decided to do *immeasurably more* (John 6:1–15).

He cast aside boundaries and expectations and performed a miracle that fed everyone there, even though the math didn't line up.

- When faced with a demon-possessed man (Mark 5:1–20), Jesus did not step back and hide behind human limitations. He showed that He lived in the realm of the *immeasurably more* and drove out the demon.

- Jesus went to Calvary and then rose from the dead. He was not confined by a body of clay or a life measured in seconds, minutes, days, months, and years. He lived in the context of eternity—the *immeasurably more*.

This book is about living in the immeasurably more. It's about casting aside those boundaries, limitations, and calculations and embracing a life that isn't easily explained. It's about understanding that there is more to life.

To do this, we will look at two passages in the Bible. Ephesians 3:14–21 and 2 Peter 1:5–7 take us outside of ourselves and usher us into a realm beyond the scales and yardsticks of our defined understanding of life. Before we begin, there is a key understanding we must have about the dynamics of living in the realm of the immeasurably more. *Living in the immeasurably more requires moving from the confines of self to life in the expanse of God.* That thought alone can be a little overwhelming, but you will soon find that the more you move away from yourself and into the center of His presence and family, the easier it will be to approach life from His perspective.

*Living in the immeasurably more requires
moving from the confines of self to life in
the expanse of God.*

Being centered in Him can be a challenge. Our natural tendency is to position ourselves so that we win arguments, appear confident, and protect our best interests. Much like a salesperson giving a presentation, we do everything we can to appear that we are in control and have life figured out. Political candidates excel at this. Athletes use this against their opponents. Men and women use it to attract spouses. The way we position ourselves matters quite a bit.

So, what would happen if we were to position ourselves in the center of God's presence? How do you position yourself in the midst of infinity? How do you center yourself in One who has no boundaries?

You may bristle at this thought. Perhaps for you, "positioning yourself in God's presence" means a checklist of rules and regulations. You imagine being placed in a spiritual straitjacket, where you are given limited movement and freedom.

This perspective only skims the surface of what God has for you. It sets you up to become worn out by the hard road that you believe is the path to heaven when God's intention is to invigorate and empower you.

The *immeasurably more* is not a straitjacket or a list of rules. It's a place where the impossible becomes possible and the rules no longer provide the power. God cannot be contained, hemmed in, or measured. He cannot be defined, corralled, or tethered. *The center of God's expanse is not found in the rules. It's found in the relationship you have with Christ and His church.*

My hope is that this book will remind you of who God

is, what He did for you through Jesus Christ, and what the Christian life is supposed to look like. At the end of each chapter, I have included a workbook section that I hope will encourage you to dig deeper into your faith, to learn more about Christ, to get into His Word, and to own your faith. When you do that, you will realize what God can truly give you. He can do immeasurably more than you can imagine. There is *more* to life than you ever thought possible!

CHAPTER ONE

The Foundation of Our Faith

As a kid, do you remember daydreaming about what you were going to be when you grew up? Maybe you wanted to be a doctor or an athlete, a police officer or a teacher. Then somewhere along the line, you realized that this question never really goes away. Even in adulthood, we tend to wonder what's in store for us once we reach some measure of maturity.

It's great to dream about the future, but how often do we hold ourselves back, assuming that it is not the right time to tackle the dreams and ambitions we have? This mindset of "not yet" can cause us to miss the "now" of what God desires to do in us. We can become so focused on tomorrow that we miss what God is doing today to *prepare* us for tomorrow.

Character Building

Regardless of our age, we are in a constant developmental process as the Lord puts building blocks of character into our lives. Those building blocks are essential to establish a strong godly foundation. When we ignore what God is trying to do in our lives, when we prevent Him from working in us, we become vulnerable to falling on our spiritual faces.

Think about when a little child goes into the playroom and builds a tower with blocks. That tower teeters back and forth, possessing the strength of a styrofoam post. The toddler is just as wobbly, and it's only a matter of time before the tower or the toddler falls down.

When we move through life without the proper foundation, we are just as unstable. I have seen lives crumble in an instant. People who seem to have it all together lose everything without notice. They are left with nothing but their skill set, and their skills are not up to the task of helping them to reach the immeasurably more that God has for them. What we need is a godly character.

Since we are created human beings, it is imperative for each one of us to address the issues of character in his or her heart. We want to have the kind of character that demonstrates that Jesus Christ is not just a word in our vocabulary. He is not merely a part of a church we attend, but rather an active part of our lives.

God works to build our character from the ground up so that no matter what life throws at us, we stay strong in Him. He takes our human blocks of failure, mistakes, and sin, and He replaces them over time with healthy, holy blocks that are steadfast and strong. These are true blocks of character, and He expects us to build with them.

The foundation God lays within us is not meant to be ignored or left alone. It is upon that foundation that God will build. When my wife and I built our house, it was not enough to have the foundation. We needed walls, electricity, plumbing, and a roof. We were not satisfied with our home until it was *complete*. The same is true of God. He builds a foundation so that He can live in us and our character may continue to grow to completion.

The first chapter of 2 Peter gives good insight into the building of character:

His divine power has given us everything we need for a godly life through our knowledge of him who called us by his own glory and goodness. Through these he has given us his very great and precious promises, so that through them you may participate in the divine nature, having escaped the corruption in the world caused by evil desires.

For this very reason, make every effort to add to your faith goodness; and to goodness, knowledge; and to knowledge, self-control; and to self-control, perseverance; and to perseverance, godliness; and to godliness, mutual affection; and to mutual affection, love. For if you possess these qualities in increasing measure, they will keep you from being ineffective and unproductive in your knowledge of our Lord Jesus Christ. But whoever does not have them is nearsighted and blind, forgetting that they have been cleansed from their past sins.

Therefore, my brothers and sisters, make every effort to confirm your calling and election. For if you do these things, you will never stumble, and you will receive a rich welcome into the eternal kingdom of our Lord and Savior Jesus Christ.
                                                    —2 Peter 1:3–11

Half-Baked

I love cinnamon rolls with lots of cinnamon and sugar and icing. I don't have time for a light glaze that acts embarrassed even to be there. Cinnamon rolls should announce their presence with wafts of tantalizing aromas that cause our mouths to salivate as it sits on a plate, oozing with icing and overflowing with delectable taste. I need plenty of everything for a full-flavor experience. Have you ever eaten a half-baked cinnamon roll? If you have, then you know that no amount of icing can cover up the underdeveloped taste. It's mushy. You put that puppy in your mouth and immediately wonder, *"What's happening?"* You taste the dough, the cinnamon, the butter. All of the elements are there, yet it's terrible! Each ingredient stands on its own because they have not been baked together. The process stopped short, and you were left with a half-baked roll.

There are a lot of people who claim to be believers. There are people who claim to have walked with Christ for twenty or thirty years, but they are half-baked. They leave a bad taste in your mouth when you are around them. They do not reflect what a true believer is because they have not fully surrendered to Jesus Christ. They are poor examples of what it means to be built up in Christ.

This passage, if put into action in our lives, will not leave us half-baked. If we move in the direction it outlines and allow Christ to build upon our foundation with His blocks, we will not need to go back into the oven.

Notice what it says in verse 5 as the writer, Peter, was poised and ready to get into the building blocks of character: "For this very reason, make every effort...." The word *effort* has a sense of purpose. It comes with a determination that you are going to grab hold of something with every bit of energy you possess. Every piece of intellect that God has given you, every ounce of discernment, whatever you have, Peter was urging you to invest it in making sure that your character is reflecting the character of Jesus Christ.

*How hard we work at something
reveals our level of interest.*

During college, I saw the most beautiful woman who ever walked the face of the earth, a Helen of Troy right there on my campus! I felt the Holy Spirit speak to me, saying, "Tom, this woman needs to know a future man of the cloth." Of course, I responded, "Here I am, Lord. Send me!"

I went to the registrar's office to find out her schedule so that when she came out of class, it would appear that I was there by divine providence. I worked and worked to get her attention and impress her. She captured my attention. She filled my thoughts. I was *consumed.* Eventually this beautiful woman became my wife, Queenie! I worked hard for her because I was completely taken with her.

We have a friend who went to medical school in Korea. This friend was telling us about how the Korean people are very disciplined. He knew of a woman who had been a Buddhist for years. The day she made a decision to walk with Jesus Christ and surrender her life, she adjusted everything she did to be focused on Him—her prayer time, her actions, her schedule. She said, "If I would get up early to spend time with Buddha, could I do any less for Christ, who is real?"

Some time after her conversion, martial law was enforced on the city. All of the churches were shut down, and people were stuck at home. When martial law was lifted, the pastor of her church decided to celebrate by holding service at 5 a.m. every morning, and she made sure that her boys attended those services. She was passing on to them the value and priority of honoring Christ. In America, there would be an uprising among church attenders if we were to hold church at 5 a.m. daily, but this woman felt that it was the least she could do to thank God for staying with her family in such difficult times.

There are a lot of things in life that consume our time, thoughts, and energy, and I guarantee that most of these things have nothing to do with Christ. I think about my day, my routine, and the things that I dwell on. I spend so much time and attention on things that don't matter to God and don't contribute to eternity, and I am sure that you see similar patterns in your own life.

It's time for us to change and move into the realm of the immeasurably more. We are to make *every effort* to build upon the foundation that God is instilling within us. This is because our effort reveals not only our level of interest, but also our level of love.

It's one thing to say that you are a Christian. It's another thing to live with Christ as the King of your life, to fall in love with Him, and to be consumed with thoughts of Him. It's one thing to ask God to clean up your mess so that you can keep going down the same path, but it's another thing to seek deep life change and to allow His building blocks to make you into a new person.

Investing in the Future

As the passage goes on, there is a distinct flow and direction to Peter's words. He said to "make every effort to add…" (2 Peter 1:5). When I see the word *add*, it takes me back to elementary school arithmetic, yet the word *add* is one of the most dynamic words that shows up in verse 5 of this scripture. It's a call to action.

In ancient Greece, the State paid for actors to perform for its citizens. A *choregos* was a wealthy citizen who helped to make these productions more lavish.[1] These individuals would *add* to what the State was already providing in an attempt to go all out with costumes, music, and more. Their goal was to impress the king and nobles. In fact, the word *choregein* became a verb known to mean "lavishly to pour out everything that is necessary for a noble performance."[2]

In this passage, the Greek word used for *add* is *epichoregein*, and it is telling us to make every effort to be lavish and excessive. William Barclay put it this way: "Peter urges his people to equip their lives with every virtue; and that equipment must not be simply a necessary minimum, but lavish and generous."[3] We are to work as though at any moment, we may be called before the king to perform.

Second Peter 1:3 reads, "His divine power has *given us everything* we need for a godly life through our knowledge of him who called us by his own glory and goodness" (emphasis added).

The verse tells us that God has already been lavish and excessive. He has held nothing back. His divine power has given us everything we need for success. The least we can do is to give our best effort and perform at our best.

I remember back in grade school when we would "fall in like" with somebody. We would write notes and have our friends pass them to the intended party, or we would send our best friend in to feel out the situation. "Hey, Tom! Barb likes you. Do you like her?" Before we knew it, our futures would be arranged without requiring us to speak face to face. We would broker engagements via third-party communications, and we would break up the same way. These were no-contact relationships.

For many of us, this is exactly how we function in our spiritual walk. We go to church and say to the guy up front, "Do you have a message from God for me?" If we don't get something we like that Sunday, we go home and assume that God didn't have anything for us. Maybe next week. We expect the pastor, the teacher, or some spiritual leader to do the digging for us. No need to check with God. No, we carry on the same no-contact relationship with Jesus that we did with the little girl or boy in grade school.

This scripture does away with that. *You* are to make the effort. *You* are to get involved. *You* are to build upon your character and add to it. *You* make contact with Christ and build on that relationship.

We like the emotion and excitement of being with Christ, but once those feelings pass, believers often lose their zeal because they never invest in the relationship. They make no effort to grow, no effort to add to their faith, so it all fades away.

Queenie and I have been married for forty-seven years. There were times when our backs were to the wall and our emotions were scattered around the room like shattered glass, but we made it through because we invested in our relationship. We put in the work. We *added* to it year after year, and forty-seven years later, I can still say that I love being married to her. I enjoy my wife. I love being with her. A marriage that does not grow, learn, and invest in connecting with each other is destined to fail, and the same goes with our relationship with Christ.

Philippians 2:12 says to "continue to work out your salvation with fear and trembling." This is serious stuff! How often do we approach it this way? When you go to church, are you just a body that fills the seat, or are you investing your heart, soul, and mind? When you go to work, are you filtering your day through the presence of Christ, or is He an afterthought until Sunday rolls around? Are you pursuing God more than you expect Him to pursue you?

Many of us think that pursuing God means doing big, bold things for Him. We think that it means martyrdom or selling all of our possessions, but it's really about small actions throughout the day, every day. Fred Craddock, in an address to ministers, caught the practical implications of this pursuit. He said:[4]

> We think giving our all to the Lord is like taking a $1,000 bill and laying it on the table—"Here's my life, Lord. I'm giving it all."
>
> But the reality for most of us is that he sends us to the bank and has us cash in the $1,000 for quarters. We go

through life putting out 25 cents here and 50 cents there. Listen to the neighbor kid's troubles instead of saying, "Get lost." Go to a committee meeting. Give a cup of water to a shaky old man in a nursing home.

Usually giving our life to Christ isn't glorious. It's done in all those little acts of love, 25 cents at a time. It would be easy to go out in a flash of glory; it's harder to live the Christian life little by little over the long haul.

This is what it means to *add*. Little by little, bit by bit, we add to our foundation with a daily, sacrificial pursuit. The result of these small additions is that they build faith.

The Definition of Faith

For this very reason, make every effort to add to your faith....
—*2 Peter 1:5*

In our culture, *faith* can mean almost anything. It can mean any religion or belief in something. I could say that I have faith in my car. In that case, my faith would be as dynamic, alive, and powerful as my car. It would also be limited by my car's capabilities. Our faith, no matter where we place it, is as dynamic, strong, and alive as its object.

However, when Peter wrote this passage, he was not referring to a nebulous object of faith. He was talking about something concrete: our relationship with Jesus Christ. Peter knew what it was like to deny Jesus (Matthew 26:69–75). He knew the agony that came with it. Out of that experience, his faith became more focused.

*Peter understood that faith was
more than hanging out with Jesus;
it was standing up for Jesus as well.*

He realized that Christ was the foundation for every-thing, and he saw the importance of building upon one's faith in a real and practical way.

Sometimes we make the mistake of assuming that faith should be an emotional experience. We get hyped up and lose ourselves in the songs, the prayers, and the message. We leave church and say, "Wow! All my emotions were stirred. God was there!" We often love the emotion of the moment so much that we fail to come away with anything tangible. We fail to add to our faith. Instead, we come away with an expectation that emotion proves that God is real. When our emotions are fired up, we say, "God was there today!" I have news for you: God is there all the time. The reality is that when we are moved, *we* are the ones who finally showed up, but it's not simply emotions that need to be stirred.

Please note that this passage does not say to make every effort to add to your emotions. Emotions ebb and flow based on circumstance while true faith remains intact regardless of the circumstances. Emotions wear us out, but faith builds us up. Emotions can cloud the issues, but faith scours the mind. Faith makes us wrestle with what we hear, and it clarifies the truth. Emotions rise on change, but faith is grounded in the one who is the same yesterday, today, and forever: Jesus Christ. This is why we are to add to our *faith*.

Adding to Faith

One of my heroes was my grandfather, my dad's dad. He was bent over and partially paralyzed in that position. He could not turn his head, but he could walk with crutches. He had rheumatoid arthritis but ultimately died of cancer. My grandfather suffered physically throughout his entire life.

Despite his physical problems, we had a ball with my grandfather. He would get up early in the morning, and he would have us kids get up, too. He would flip our cots to wake us up! Sometimes he would poke me with his crutch to get me out of bed. It was all in fun, and it made waking up early more fun than it would have been otherwise.

My grandfather loved the Lord with all of his heart, but he had not always been a Christian. I did not know him in those days, but Dad filled in the gaps. The day came when my grandfather made the decision to walk with Jesus Christ. From that moment on, he was serious about his faith. At the time, his boys (my dad and his brothers) were not walking with God. Every night, my grandfather would painfully go up the steps of the house to pray with his boys. The whole process took him two hours, but he was sincere about teaching his boys about Christ, so he made the trip—every night.

Suddenly the faith that was so real to my grandfather became real to my dad. My dad went off to college and met my mom, who was also serious about her faith. They got married and had my brother, my sister, and me, and just like their parents before them, they made every effort to invest in us.

The faith that had become my grandfather's became my father's and, eventually, mine. Although my grandfather is now in heaven, I am connected to him because of my faith in the Lord. I am talking to the same God, believing in the same Christ.

As a result, Queenie and I made every effort to invest in our kids. I would be lying if I told you that it was always a smooth ride, but over time, our faith—the faith of my grandfather and my father before me—became the faith of our daughter and the faith of our son. Both of them are pastors today.

It is never too much work to instill faith in yourself and those around you. The devil tells us something different. He affects our thinking and deceives us into believing that it's a lost cause or it's too hard. The Bible does not shy away from this. It will take *effort*, yet we are to do it. It's imperative that we add to our faith day by day. This is the first building block from which we can begin to experience the *immeasurably more* of life.

WORKBOOK

Chapter One Questions

Question: Looking at how you spend your time and energy, is there evidence to reveal the level of your love for Christ? What do your habits and routines reveal about your level of interest and love? Do you need to change your lifestyle in order to make every effort to add to your faith daily?

_____

_____

_____

_____

_____

_____

_____

_____

Question: Are you digging into your relationship with Christ on your own, or are you relying on pastors, teachers, or other spiritual leaders to do the digging for you? Do you find yourself going to church and expecting a message from your pastor or someone else that reignites your fire for God, or do you take responsibility for making every effort to keep your connection with Christ? If you are depending too much on others to do the work for you, what changes do you need to make?

_____

_____

_____

_____

_____

_____

_____

_____

_____

_____

Question: What does faith mean to you? What do you think is the evidence of faith? How do you know when you have faith? Do you depend on an emotional sensation to make you feel like you are full of faith and close to God? What else can be an indicator of your faith? How can you walk in faith even when you do not feel it?

_____

_____

_____

_____

_____

_____

_____

_____

_____

_____

_____

_____

_____

Action: *It will take effort, yet we are to do it. It's impera-tive that we add to our faith day by day.* Intentionally make an effort to add to your faith daily. Ask God to show you what this looks like for you. What small steps can you take to move in that direction? Here's an example of how you can be intentional about adding to your faith every day:

1. Invest time every day in prayer and Bible study.

2. Do something for Christ that requires faith and not just your skills, something that forces you to step beyond your comfort zone.

3. Share your faith with others.

4. Look at the faith of those who are serving Christ around you. Learn from them and be inspired by them.

Chapter One Notes

_____

_____

_____

_____

_____

_____

_____

_____

_____

_____

_____

_____

_____

_____

_____

_____

_____

_____

_____

_____

_____

_____

_____

CHAPTER TWO

The Characteristics of Faith

The best pieces of meatloaf are the thick ones in the middle. Are you with me? Sure, the heels are fine, but if you are serving and asking me which I prefer, I am going to say "the middle piece" every time. Sometimes we treat Scripture the same way. We choose what we think are the superior pieces. We look at 2 Peter 1:5–7 and say, "I'll take self-control," or, "Give me a good slice of perseverance." We approach Scripture as if we can pick and choose the characteristics we want, thinking that there is no way we can handle the full loaf.

Second Peter 1:5–7 is not a pick-and-choose passage. Every single one of these building blocks of character is essential for every single believer. No exceptions. No picking and choosing.

For this very reason, make every effort to add to your faith goodness; and to goodness, knowledge; and to knowledge, self-control; and to self-control, perseverance; and to perseverance, godliness; and to godliness, mutual affection; and to mutual affection, love.
—2 Peter 1:5–7

There is a logical progression in the way these characteristics unfold. As we walk through them, I hope you will see that in everything God does, He has a design. If we allow that design to unfold in the manner He intends, we will be amazed at how we blossom.

The first two characteristics, goodness and knowledge, help to build up our faith.

Goodness

When I think of goodness, my default is to assume that a good person is also a bland person, someone who lacks intrigue and personality. Good equals vanilla. That is not remotely what this passage is saying!

The New Testament was written primarily in Koine Greek. The Greek word used for *goodness* in this passage is *aretē*. This word is filled with meaning and comes with a sense of moral goodness and God's power.[5] This word goes around flexing its muscles because there is strength to it. It has the ability to *do*, to be effective. It's active.

In New Testament Scripture, the writers would often draw word-pictures for us. The better we become acquainted with the Scriptures, the better we will understand these word-pictures. The word *arétē* was often used to refer to the kind of farmland that was rich and fertile as far as the eye could see. It was the kind of land that was destined to produce many crops. This is the picture that the passage is trying to paint for the reader. We need to be fertile soil for the character of Christ to grow in us.

The word for *goodness* in the Greek also speaks of a moral power. William Barclay described this type of person as an "expert in the technique of living well."[6] This person has it all together, but the word also hints at another characteristic: *motivation*. This kind of goodness speaks of an inner motivation.

There's a song we sing around Christmas time called *Santa Claus Is Comin' to Town*:[7]

> Oh you better watch out, you better not cry, you better not pout I'm telling you why. Santa Claus is coming to town. He knows when you've been sleeping, he knows when you're awake, he knows when you've been bad or good so be good for goodness' sake.

What a bunch of garbage! I challenge you to find one kid who will be good "for goodness' sake" around Christmas time. All the kids I know are good for presents' sake! They obey because it means that they will find gifts under the tree, not because of a deep desire to be good. However, if we examine the intent of Scripture, being good for goodness' sake is exactly what this passage says.

Jesus said that no one is good other than God (Mark 10:18). That being the case, my desire to be good does not grow out of the fact that I expect God to lavish gifts on me or to reward me in all kinds of ways. Instead, I am to be good for *His* sake. I am to be motivated in my heart because of my love for Him. How many of us are honestly living this out?

Think of it this way: A man and his buddy go into a convenience store. Just as they walk in, the place gets robbed. The robber is stealing from all the patrons in the store. The two men are backed up against the wall, and suddenly one guy starts nudging the other guy. The guy being nudged says, "Don't try to give me a gun. I don't want to be a hero!" His friend says, "It's not a gun. It's the twenty-five bucks I owe you."

What impeccable timing, right? The man was not motivated to pay back his debt until he was about to lose it. That is how many of us treat God. The only reason we give something to the Lord is because someone sticks an offering plate in front of us. The only reason we teach Sunday school is because we kept getting pestered about it until we gave in. The only reason we run tech or clean the building or manage the bookkeeping is because no one else wants to do it. Very few of us serve for the sake of the Lord. We serve out of obligation or because we believe that we will get a reward when all is said and done.

The passage here reads, "...add to your faith goodness" (2 Peter 1:5). I describe goodness as the inner motivation, the inner drive to serve the Lord purely out of desire and love. It's when you say, "I'm going to be good, not because I'm afraid of getting caught or of the consequences or because I want to get something good in return, but because I'm in love with Jesus Christ." In other words, goodness does not grow out of fear or entitlement. It grows out of faith and that pure inner desire for Jesus Christ.

Courage

There is something else essential built into the word *arété*. This word comes with courage.[8] When I first started examining this passage, I could not reconcile the two. How could *goodness* also come with *courage*? My own preconceived notion was that goodness is a one-way ticket to Weakness City; it's not bold or daring. However, the original Greek is clear that goodness comes with courage.

The Scriptures say that when we give our lives to Jesus Christ, we are transformed. We start to change. Most people I know struggle with change because it takes us outside of our comfort zone. Change causes us to do things that are not the norm. Therefore, the idea of being transformed is intimidating, and some of us resist it.

I have seen women marry men who are abusive or alcoholics. The marriage is terrible, and the woman finally leaves, only to jump into another bad relationship with the same kind of man. Part of the problem is that she does not know how to function outside of what she already knows. Change is scary, so she reverts back to what is comfortable—comfortable, yet potentially devastating.

Most of us are the same way. Regardless of the pattern that has been instilled in our lives or how we have learned to relate, change is difficult and requires courage. When Christ comes along and says that we need goodness, He is saying that we need courage to change. We need courage to dare to be good in a world that lacks goodness.

Married couples wrestle with this. Two people coming together from different backgrounds and lifestyles surrender to one another in a sacred union. Then the differences between them begin to surface—spending habits, personal hygiene practices, dietary preferences, you name it—and those differences mean that they need to change! Those changes create tension because life is not the way it used to be.

Change is hard. Do you know why married couples fight over things that are minor? Change rocks their security base. However, when we give our lives to Christ, He says that *He* is our rock, our foundation. We need to look to Him and allow Him to give us courage to change in the manner that He wants us to change, knowing that our true security is found only in Him, not in our habits, routines, or false idols.

Think about your business or work. When you make decisions, what is your bottom line? Is it profit, or is it the testimony you are going to leave the person with whom you are dealing?

When you interact with your spouse, what is your bottom line? Is it winning the fight, or is it having a relationship that is whole, holy, and sound? When you deal with your children, what motivates you in the area of discipline? Is discipline a way for you to express anger, or do you desire a healthy interaction with your children that will help to mold them in the manner that Christ wants to mold them?

When you are tempted, do you look for the way of escape that the Lord promised, or do you look for excuses and justifications to go ahead and sin? Each and every one of these scenarios requires courage to choose what is right rather than what is comfortable, convenient, and self-gratifying.

We used to live in Kansas, and there is a story about a couple who moved there long ago when it was considered the Wild West.[9] We will call this couple Greg and Becky. They found some land, settled down, and built a home. The man of the house, Greg, would leave for long periods of time to hunt. He installed a bell and told Becky, "If ever there is an emergency or something terrible staring you in the face, ring that bell, and I'll be there."

One day when Greg was out on a hunt, he heard the bell. He rushed back to the house as fast as he could, and Becky said, "Greg! When are you going to hang the clothesline so I can get the wash out?"

Greg looked at her, a little stunned. "I said to ring the bell if it's an emergency!" You could tell that he was a little irritated, but he got back on his horse and went out hunting.

A little bit later, he heard the bell a second time. He charged back home and found Becky, who said, "Greg! When are you going to build a fence to keep the chickens in?"

Smoke billowed from Greg's ears. His face turned red. "I told you not to ring the bell if it's not an emergency!" By this time, Greg's holiness was fading fast.

He got back on his horse and went out to hunt. A little bit later, he heard the bell a third time. He hurried to the house and found that it had been burned to the ground. Everything was gone, and Becky had an arrow in her arm. He charged over to her, pulled her up, and said, "Now that's more like it."

It's a silly analogy, but this is exactly the way most of us respond to Jesus Christ. We say, "Lord, if You have something really important out there, call me. Otherwise, don't mess with me." God calls, and we say, "You know, that opportunity doesn't interest me. It's not that important. Get back to me when You have something really good, okay?"

That's how we live our lives. We tell God that we are on call 24/7, but when He calls, we have a predetermined idea of what is and is not worthy of our response. I am here to tell you that this is not biblical goodness. There is no power to it. It's ineffective and unproductive, and it shows a lack of courage.

That's why at the very onset of building on this foundation of faith, the Bible says to "make every effort to add to your faith goodness" (2 Peter 1:5)—strength of character. This inner motivation makes us ready and anxious to do whatever God asks us to do, knowing that by the power of the Holy Spirit, we can be effective and productive for His glory.

Knowledge

It's not enough simply to have zeal or to be ready to charge out of the gates with goodness and courage if we don't know where we are going, so the Bible commands us to add to goodness *gnósis*, or knowledge.[10] There are different words for knowledge in the Greek, but this particular word indicates a practical knowledge.[11] In other words, it's something you know by virtue of experience. It's a hands-on kind of knowledge. It's not picking up a textbook and looking up the word or learning by instruction and academics. It's a knowledge that has been tested and experienced.

It's important that we understand the role of knowledge

in our quest to go deeper with God. Knowledge moves us beyond the superficial. Our relationships with people often do not move far beyond casual conversation. We have surface interactions, which keep our relationships superficial. That is not where we want to be with God. We need to know Him.

I believe that one of the struggles in the church today is that fewer and fewer people have a hands-on knowledge of God. For many, their spiritual knowledge is all secondhand. They take what they get from their pastor or their parents, and that's it. They do not delve into the person and character of Christ. To them, Jesus embodies a religion and not much more.

Truly knowing God provides a doorway through which we can fall more deeply in love with Christ. This particular type of knowledge means that to know God is to experience God. Knowing God helps us to understand the bigger picture. Life can sometimes close in on us, and all we see is our crisis or what we perceive to be our opportunities. Knowing God brings a holy and broader perspective, giving guidance and insight so we can see beyond the moment.

Knowing God enables us to be discerning, seeing beyond our own desires and merging our lives with the desires of God.

When that occurs, we discover the depth of the grace and peace offered to us by our heavenly Father. We are not simply reading about grace and peace, but actually owning them because we know God and we know that He is giving these things to us. When we recognize that His grace is ours and always available, our confidence in our relationship with Christ increases.

How do we exercise *knowledge* and get to know God? This is done through knowing His Word and applying it to our everyday lives. Absorbing the truths of Scripture provides a hedge of protection and an inner light to keep us from stumbling into a life of sin. Scripture also works with His Spirit living inside of us. The two provide irreplaceable knowledge for how to handle and navigate life. When I look at Queenie, I wonder what on earth possessed us to get married. You see, the love we had for one another the day we were married is nothing compared to the level of love we have now. In retrospect, that young love seems so incomplete and shallow. It pales in comparison to the love we have today, a love that has deepened and grown as we have gotten to know one another and experienced the good and the bad of life together. God wants to have a similar journey with each of us.

When it comes to love, we like excitement. We like it when our palms sweat and our hearts race, but true love is so much more than these fleeting emotions. Compare it to the ocean. Where do ocean waves break? They break on the shore, in the shallows. When you move farther into the deep, the waves are not breaking as much, but there is a lot more to explore. After forty-seven years, my palms do not sweat as much when I see Queenie, but the relationship is far deeper than it has ever been.

A relationship built purely on appearance or superficial interaction is going to fade as time goes by. This type of relationship floats out into the deep end without knowing how to swim. A relationship built upon knowing one another on a deeper, more intimate level is one that knows how to navigate deep waters, storms, and crashing waves. When I look in the mirror every day, it scares me. I have lines and wrinkles and bumps and skin spots, and it's horrible! However, my relationship with Queenie is not stuck in the shallows. We are in over our heads in the depths!

It's not how we look, but rather who we are that forms the foundation of our mutual love. We *know* each other. The reason a lot of believers drift is because they never bother to explore their relationship with Jesus Christ. They chase after sweaty palms, a racing heart, and fired-up emotions. The moment the music dies down and these feelings fade away, they question the validity of their walk with God. This is because they do not know how to swim in the depths of life with Christ.

If my emotions were to dictate my relationship with Queenie, then I would be questioning our marriage every time we have a boring weekend together or a difficult season. Imagine if every time I got a headache, I immediately thought, *"This isn't what I signed up for! I thought marriage was supposed to provide a solution to my problems! I must not be married!"* What a dumb conclusion that would be, yet many people draw that kind of conclusion about their relationship with Christ. If things are not going well, they conclude that they should not be Christians or that God must not care about them.

My relationship with Queenie is built upon my knowledge of her, and I know that a boring weekend or some hardship or a headache does not mean that she loves me any less or that we are not meant for one another. Too often, we do not give the Lord the same benefit of the doubt. We start to feel lousy, defeated, or bored, and it makes us question the validity of our Christianity or, even worse, the validity of Christ. When we *know* Jesus, we are not insecure in the relationship. We have *experienced* Him at work in our lives and through Scripture.

Do you know what I love about my home? I can go there, curl up on the couch in the fetal position, and cry like a baby, and I know that Queenie is going to love me just the same. I am secure in her love for me because I know her. We need the same type of relationship with God. We need to get acquainted with the Lord until we know Him so well that we feel we can curl up and have a moment without Him blinking an eye.

Knowing God also gives us confidence in His will for our lives. Part of our problem is that we want to know His will without knowing Him. It doesn't work that way.

When I was growing up, my personality was such that I would talk about everything and anything. It did not matter; I would just throw it all out on the table. Even though I would talk about anything, there were certain things that I never asked my parents. Do you know why? Because I knew what they would say. How did I know what my parents would say? Because I lived with them every single day, and I knew how they thought.

To know God's will, we must live with Jesus every single day and dive into His Scripture and listen to the Spirit. That is why we add knowledge to goodness. That intimate knowledge gives us experience with God and security and direction for life. The more I know God, the more insight I will have into what He wants me to do and who He is and who I am. That's an experiential type of knowledge. It's a full and intimate knowledge.

Conviction

Knowing God also brings conviction. Conviction is a sense of morality, a sense of being convinced that something is right or wrong. It's an inner judgment that comes from the knowledge of what God defines as right and wrong.

I have found that the better I know Him, the better I understand what matters in life. Through this lens, I am able to stay in the center of where I need to be. I become convicted of things that fall outside of God's presence and His best for my life.

One of the things that we lack in the church is conviction, and that is because we do not enter the presence of

God. We do not *know* Him, so people come to church week after week, and nothing changes. Their minds and hearts are elsewhere, and they continue with life as if nothing happened. What's more, when people do not know God, they are easily pulled into false teachings and doctrines. They have no way to sift or measure what they are told, so they take everything at face value. This is how we end up with bizarre preachers whose teaching is not at all rooted in Scripture, yet their followers buy into it because it feeds their personal appetites rather than God's desires.

Knowing God means knowing what He is about. It means measuring what you are told against what you know to be true of Scripture and the nature of God. It means being convicted when things are off-center.

Security

Knowing God means being secure in your relationship with Him. Too many people live their lives afraid that at any moment, God is going to remove them from His Book of Life, but that's not the way it works. Willful, continued disobedience is what you need to look out for; it's a choice.

Do you think that in forty-seven years, Queenie and I have never had a disagreement? We have had more than I can count! We could have chosen divorce. We could have chosen separation. Instead, our love compelled us to come together to restore the relationship. When we know God, we understand that one bad moment does not ruin it for us. He is in it for the long haul, but only if we choose to stick around.

When I was a child living in Pennsylvania, we were heading out as a family when my dad said that he needed to stop at the mailbox to drop off some mail. The mailbox was at the end of the street, so we drove down the lane and stopped.

I insisted on being the one to drop the mail into the mailbox. I begged and begged until finally my dad handed me the mail and gave me the typical fatherly lecture. The box was across the street from where the car was parked, and he wanted to make sure that I would be safe.

"Now, Tom, make sure to walk to the front of the car and look both ways before crossing the street," he said.

"I know. I know." I waved him off and jumped out of the car. Instead of crossing in front of the car, I went to the back. Instead of looking both ways, I just darted out into the street!

About that same time, our neighbor was rounding the corner in her car. She hit me, knocking me back to the curb. I was out cold. Do you think that my parents yelled, "You should have listened!" and drove off without me? Do you think that they let me lie there and suffer? Not a chance. The moment the car hit me, my parents bolted from the vehicle and rushed to my side.

Knowing God means knowing that even when we sin and fall on our faces, He is there with us. He rushes to our aid and wants nothing more than for us to learn from our mistakes and do better next time. As you continue to add to your building blocks, as you continue to exercise goodness and knowledge, you will have fewer moments in which you fall. Even when you do fall, you will know that God is there to pick you up when you ask.

Step by Step

There was a joke circulating around the internet for a while about three guys who were out fishing.[12] One guy got bored, stepped out of the boat, and walked across the water to the shore. Soon another guy was equally bored, so he also left the boat and walked across the water to the shore.

The last guy in the boat did not like being alone, so he got out and immediately sank to the bottom of the lake! He got back into the boat and tried again—and again. Three times he stepped out of the boat, and three times he sank.

Watching this, the two guys on shore turned to one another and wondered aloud, "Should we tell him where the stepping stones are?"

Some people have this great ability to weather difficult times. They lose a spouse or face horrible adversity, and they keep going, seemingly unfazed. Let me tell you something: these are the people who know where the stones are. They know where to step; they know how to keep their heads above water.

Knowing God is knowing where to step.

Goodness is being compelled to take that step in faith for the glory of God. When you find yourself in difficult situations, He leads you to safety. He brings you back to the center. You can move with confidence, no matter what is going on around you, because you know the bigger picture.

> For this very reason, make every effort to add to your faith goodness....
> —2 Peter 1:5

We need that inner courage and motivation to keep going, that desire to be effective for the King.

...and to goodness, knowledge....

—2 Peter 1:5

Then we add an experiential understanding that Jesus Christ Himself died on the cross for us. He knows us, and He is unfolding a divine plan for you and for me. These building blocks of faith are foundational to us stepping into a life of the immeasurably more. They are absolutely necessary for getting in sync with God's plan and keeping our faith rooted. These two blocks are just the beginning of discovering the *more* to life.

WORKBOOK

Chapter Two Questions

Question: Why do you do good things? Ask the Holy Spirit to help you discern the motives behind your good behavior. Are you trying to impress others? Are you trying to earn a reward from God? Are you doing something in hopes of getting something in return or to avoid certain consequences, or is your goodness rooted in love for Jesus and a desire for Him alone? Be honest with God about this and allow Him to purify your motives behind the good things you do.

_____

_____

_____

_____

_____

_____

_____

_____

_____

_____

_____

Question: What does it mean to know God? What does it mean to know Him through experience? Have you experienced God? Do you experience Him daily? If not, do you want to know Him through experience? What changes do you need to make in order to position yourself to experience true, intimate relationship with God?

_____

_____

_____

_____

_____

_____

_____

_____

_____

_____

_____

Question: Do you feel secure or fearful in your relationship with God? Do you feel like you have to keep up performances before God in order for Him to accept you, or do you feel free enough to be real about your weaknesses and mistakes? Only time can build that trust and security, so when you find yourself struggling, go to God. Experience His faithfulness and the trust that comes from knowing Him.

_____

_____

_____

_____

_____

_____

_____

_____

_____

_____

_____

Action: *How do we exercise **knowledge** and get to know God? This is done through knowing His Word and applying it to our everyday lives.* You have to start somewhere, and the best place to start getting to know God is through His Word. If this is new to you, start small. Make an intentional choice to spend time in God's Word and in prayer for a window of time that feels manageable and is not overwhelming. The more you invest in your relationship with God, the more natural it will become and the more you will be able to build on your foundation of knowing Him.

Chapter Two Notes

_____

_____

_____

_____

_____

_____

_____

_____

_____

_____

_____

_____

_____

_____

_____

_____

_____

_____

_____

_____

_____

CHAPTER THREE

Breaking Sinful Patterns

Picture yourself at the end of a typical workday. You cannot wait to get home, but shortly before you are ready to leave, one of your co-workers gives you a royal tongue lashing. What do you do?

Your child comes home from school and tells you that he just flunked a major exam. Before you can say anything, he says, "And it's your fault! You made me go to bed early last night, and I had to do all these chores around the house. It's your fault that I flunked!" What do you do?

You go to an all-you-can-eat restaurant. You, being a steward of the Lord, do not want to waste your money, so you pig out! You are beyond full when a huge piece of coconut cream pie, smothered in whipped cream, is placed before you. What do you do?

You are watching TV, a show you enjoy, when an erotic scene comes onto the screen. What do you do?

You are having a conversation with somebody, and she begins to praise someone you have dirt on. You wonder, *"How can you think that person is so great?"* You want to set things straight. What do you do?

It's easy to become desensitized to sin. The culture

around us, the people with whom we spend time, the habits we form, all of these things can work to tear down our sensitivity to sin. We lash out at people. We gossip. We sit with our lust or our gluttony, and we think that what we are doing isn't that bad. Over time, our appreciation for what Christ wants us to do is no longer as solid as it once was. We begin to settle into the values of the world. Scripture says that this shouldn't happen.

In order to rise above the crowd, we need to settle into the character of Jesus Christ.

Christ's character is far from the standards of a society gone awry.

> *For this very reason, make every effort to add to your faith goodness; and to goodness, knowledge; and to knowledge, self-control; and to self-control, perseverance; and to perseverance, godliness; and to godliness, mutual affection; and to mutual affection, love.*
> **—2 Peter 1:5–7**

Do not miss something critical in this passage: simply acquiring these characteristics does not mean that you have arrived. In fact, the very next verse reads, "For if you possess these qualities *in increasing measure*, they will keep you from being ineffective and unproductive in your knowledge of our Lord Jesus Christ" (2 Peter 1:8, emphasis added). Acquiring these traits is not enough. We must allow them to blossom and grow, ever increasing.

Three of the traits speak directly to tackling sin problems: self-control, perseverance, and godliness. In this chapter, we will look at each of these building blocks and how we can allow them to develop in our own lives.

Self-Control

It's a lot easier to talk about self-control than to practice it in the events of daily life. Self-control is not an intent or an attitude. Self-control is an action. It is something we are to put into play.

Appetites and passions dominate our lives. The Greek philosopher Aristotle attempted to categorize our various responses to these passions. He wrote about *sophrosune, akolasia, akrasia,* and *egkrateia.*

According to Aristotle, we have reached *sophrosune* when reason dominates emotion. This is when you have such control over your character and soundness of mind that temptation is not even a factor.[13] (Obviously, this theory of Aristotle's is not biblically based. It does not address the concept of original sin, the fact that we were all born into sin and have committed sin.)

At the other end of the spectrum, he argued that it is possible to reach *akolasia,* in which appetite dominates reason. We would call this "unbridled lust." It's when whatever sin or temptation put before you becomes an invitation you accept. There is no self-discipline in this state. Your desires become the engine that drives your life.

In between these two extremes, Aristotle suggested two other states of mind. *Akrasia* is when your passions and reason are at war with one another. Aristotle found that in this state, passion usually wins over reason, and emotions and appetites eventually rule the day. *Egkrateia* is when your passions and reason are doing battle, but your reason wins out. We call this self-control.

The word *egkrateia* is the same Greek word that Peter used in this particular passage, but he did not use it in the context of self-mastery.[14] He used it in the context of an individual who has surrendered his or her life completely to Jesus Christ. Self-control is the evidence of a master, a Lord, who dominates our lives.

Now I want you to see how self-control fits into this passage. First, we have a foundation of faith. To that faith we add goodness, which is an inner zeal, a desire, and moral strength. It is an eagerness to get out and accomplish something for the Lord. Zeal alone will not do it, so to goodness we add knowledge. Knowledge tells us what road to take. It directs us to God and keeps us centered. Next, we are to add to knowledge self-control.

Self-control is the ability to keep your hands on the wheel while you are going down the road.

Self-control prevents distractions from pulling you off course. If you have ever driven a vehicle in an open field, you know that it's much easier to get stuck or to lose control in that type of setting. Because there are not any constraints, you don't know what is out there. You just *go*, and you end up hitting all of the bumps and obstacles along the way. As a result, it's easy to get stuck in the mud or blow a tire. No control equals a lack of safety and direction.

Knowledge comes along and says, "That's the direction you are going, and those are the boundaries." Self-control provides the constraints to stay within those boundaries and the commitment to go in that direction.

When Queenie and I lived in South Carolina, we traveled up and down Interstate 85 quite a bit. They were always working on the highway in the same manner that they work on every interstate across the nation, so they had those cement barriers in the middle of the road, a wall of concrete that made you feel closed in. Inevitably, I would be going home late at night, and it would be pouring down rain. I am an old man, and I cannot see where I am going, making that scenario particularly challenging. Then I would get stuck between a semi and the concrete wall! At that point, I had a decision to make: Should I look at the truck or the wall? Neither! I needed to be looking straight ahead. This is the secret of self-control. It means watching where you should be going, not where you shouldn't be going.

The church has made a terrible error: we spend too much time telling people what they shouldn't be doing instead of what they should be doing! We focus on the things that we "can't" do in Christianity, and pretty soon the people around us are wondering why we would ever go to church in the first place. Note how this passage in 2 Peter avoids telling us all of the things that we *shouldn't* do. Instead, it focuses only on what we *should* do.

When my son Augie (David) was eight years old, we began to study karate together. We thought this was a manly thing to do, but let me tell you that machismo is a dangerous trait to have!

One day, Queenie, Punk (Heather, my daughter), Augie, and I were on a family outing to K-Mart. Augie and I headed to electronics, where we could slobber and drool over stereos. When kids are small, it's easy to look straight over their heads, not see them, and lose track of their presence. I suddenly realized that Augie was gone.

I went aisle after aisle, looking for him. Finally, I saw him walking toward me, and a plan popped into my brain. I walked up to him, screamed in my best karate yell, and turned as if to kick him in the stomach. I did not follow through with the kick. I stopped in front of his stomach, then turned and walked away. As I took a turn down another aisle, there was Augie.

I quickly looked back at the kid I had pretended to do a karate move on, and he was moving away from me—fast. At that moment, the Holy Spirit told me to get out of K-Mart. For days, I had visions of the boy's family showing up in church and him saying, "Mom! That's the guy!"

Had I taken the time to be aware of my surroundings, I would have realized that the boy I was pretending to kick was not Augie. A little bit of knowledge would have gone a long way.

This is how knowledge fits with self-control: knowledge gives us direction, and self-control gives us restraint. Self-control is the commitment to go where God is leading you, to pursue the goal with such intent that you can ignore or do not even notice the distractions along the way.

We improve our knowledge when we add the building block of self-control and our focus is so clear that we only see the goal, the prize, the immeasurably more.

One of our problems is that we tend to be less consumed by the goal and more consumed by the distractions. We spend more time feeding our minds with screens of all types and all the other media that is available and less time in His Word, less time understanding what He has to say, less time committing His Word to memory so that when we hit a crisis, He can navigate us through it.

Perseverance

...and to self-control, perseverance; and to perseverance, godliness....

—2 Peter 1:6

Knowledge and self-control are nearly useless if we do not have the ability to persevere when the world comes against us. *Perseverance* is the Greek word *hupomone,* and it comes with a lot of insight built into the word.[15] First and foremost, the word conveys a sense of vision, the ability to see beyond the crisis.

I have talked to a lot of people who have felt battered by life and have expressed, "I've had enough. I can't take any more. I'm at the end of my rope." Let's face it: most of us have felt that way at one time or another in our lives. If one more bad thing happens, we don't know how we are going to handle it. The pain is too great!

However, there is a huge difference between trying to endure hardship by our own human will and allowing the Holy Spirit to step in and provide us with the ability to persevere. Human endurance puts up with stuff, but godly perseverance sees the bigger picture. Human endurance concentrates on the weight of the moment, but godly perseverance concentrates on the ultimate goal.

The phrase "the light at the end of the tunnel" describes *hupomone.* No matter how dark it is, the person who has godly perseverance is hopeful. This person is focused on the light, no matter how small it may seem.

Human endurance grits its teeth and waits. Godly perseverance gathers resources and walks. Even though the steps may be miniscule, godly perseverance keeps on, recognizing that God continues to be present. Godly perseverance walks forward. Human endurance labors under the "why" of the moment. Godly perseverance dwells in the wealth of God's grace.

When I am in the midst of a crisis, I do not always see that speck of light. This is where the building block of faith comes in. I know that if I just keep walking, light will show up. We cannot allow the "whys" of life to form masks and blinders around us. We need to allow God's grace to keep moving us forward. *That does not mean we do not explore the "whys"; it means that we are not stopped by them.*

Human endurance stumbles under man's frailties, but godly perseverance continues to move forward by God's faithfulness. That's what keeps us going. In fact, Christ Himself set the example. Hebrews 12:2 describes Jesus as "the founder and perfecter of our faith, who for the joy that was set before him endured the cross, despising the shame, and is seated at the right hand of the throne of God" (ESV).

Jesus had a vision beyond the moment, and this vision drove Him. He had a vision for me, for you, for all people who have ever been. His vision was an eternity spent together with us, and that vision kept Him going even when the agony and cost were great. This type of vision can be ours when we embrace the type of perseverance that the Bible is talking about, a focused hopefulness that comes from *knowing* that there is a light at the end of the tunnel.

There is something else built into *hypomonē* that is extremely profound and helps to set godly perseverance apart from human perseverance. Luke 8:15 reads, "But the seed on good soil stands for those with a noble and good heart, who hear the word, retain it, and by *persevering* produce a crop" (emphasis added).

*Godly perseverance not only makes
it through the crisis, but makes it
through the crisis and comes out
on the other side with fruit.*

If you have ever seen people go through loss or grief or extreme trials and still serve others, bring others into the Kingdom, and spread godly joy, that is perseverance. In the midst of their darkest times, they never lose sight of what is important.

It's one thing to talk about perseverance; it's another to practice it. I remember when I first started out in the ministry as a youth pastor. All youth pastors are insane. I say that with respect, but it's a fact. I was a new youth pastor, and I decided that we were going to take our youth group on a cross-country bike trip. This was all well and good, except we did nothing to prepare.

We decided that we would start our trip up around Lake Michigan and head south. We hired someone to guide us, and I told him, "Look, Craig, we're looking forward to this trip, but we haven't done anything to prepare, so cut us some slack."

He said, "No problem. We'll take it easy the first day." The first day, we did thirty-five miles. Now, that's not bad—if you are in shape. We were not. By the end of the day, riding my road bike felt like I was running in place on a fence rail. Lots of pain, lots of discomfort.

Queenie is not a high-adventure kind of woman, but she winds up doing a lot of stuff with me. I like adventure; I like experiencing new things. For her, adventure is getting lost in the pages of a great book. High adventure would be falling asleep while she is reading. This trip was not quite in her wheelhouse. I will never forget how, near the end of the first day, we were pedaling along when she started to cry.

I wanted to fix it, but I did not know how. When we stopped and set up camp, I went up to Craig. "Craig, did you forget? We're not prepared for this. We haven't trained for this."

He said, "Don't sweat it. Tomorrow we'll cut back."

The next day, we went seventy miles. By this time, I had figured out that Craig was a liar.

As we left camp on the third day, Queenie started to cry again. I was beside myself, but then I realized, *"Hey, I'm in charge here!"* Craig had spent the whole trip driving in his van, leading the way and checking on everyone, so I figured that Queenie could ride with him. Sounds reasonable, right?

Sure enough, Craig came by, and I said, "Hey, Craig, Queenie is having a tough time, and I want to put her in the van."

He shook his head. "I don't think so," he said, and he drove away. I do not want to tell you how I felt about Craig at that moment. They were not godly thoughts.

I want you to get this: the way that I felt about fixing the situation for Queenie is the same way we approach our relationship with Christ, and it gets us into trouble. We find ourselves in a difficult situation, and we want to fix it. We want it to get better, so we figure, *"I'm a Christian! God will bail me out!"* When God does not come through in the manner we want, we start to break down. *"Why isn't God saving me? Doesn't He know how much I am suffering? Doesn't He care?"*

Chapter 3 of the book of Daniel is one of those Scripture passages that seems like it should give us confidence that God will pull us out of suffering. Shadrach, Meshach, and Abednego refused to bow down to a false god. When threatened with being thrown into a fiery furnace, they said, "Do it! Our God will bail us out!" Many Christians cling to this kind of mentality, but if you keep reading the

THERE IS *MORE* TO LIFE · 55

verses, you will find that these men also said, "But either way, no matter what God chooses to do with us, we're still not going to bow down to you" (Daniel 3:18, paraphrase). When they were bound and thrown into the fire, the Bible says that the men who threw them into the fire were all killed; that's how hot the fire was. When King Nebuchadnezzar looked inside the furnace, he saw not three men in the fire, but four. The Lord Himself was there. Eventually, Nebuchadnezzar walked up to the door and invited the Hebrew men to come out, and the heat did not kill him. This indicates that the three men were in the fire long enough for it to start to die down. We tend to think that God is not going to make us stay in the fire long, but that is not true. This kind of mindset can be rooted deep in our thinking, and it causes some believers to give up in the midst of the battle because they are not prepared. They do not realize that God may keep them in the fire until it is mere embers.

This is why perseverance is so important. We *will* be in battle, so we *must* be equipped to persevere. Thinking, *"God won't make me go through this,"* is ignoring reality. Perseverance allows us to stay the course regardless of what happens. It is an essential building block for being built up in Christ.

Godliness

To perseverance, Peter next added the trait of godliness. The Greek word used in this passage is *eusebeia*,[16] which means "piety." It is not a devotional piety or something that sits on a shelf and looks sweet and holy. This form of godliness comes with community. It cannot exist independent of a relationship with others.

Eusebeia concerns not only our walk with God, but also how we relate to and interact with others. Though self-control may give us the ability to keep tempers from erupting, that alone is not sufficient. Godliness takes us beyond this to a point where, in addition to staying calm in difficult situations, we respond with mercy and grace, just as our Lord Jesus would.

I remember reading a Charles Schulz Peanuts cartoon many years ago in which the characters go back to school and are instructed to write an essay on what they did over the summer. Lucy gets up and reads what she wrote. She shares all of the junk she did and then wraps it up by saying, "But it's so good to be back within these hallowed halls of learning. Where you, my esteemed leader of Academia, stretch my mind to infinite truths and cause me to be the scholar and student that I need to be."

Lucy takes her seat beside Charlie Brown and, with a smugness only she can muster, says to him, "After a while, you know what sells."

Some of us have been around the church long enough that we know what sells, but we have forgotten what saves. We have forgotten about what transforms lives, about a Lord who is dynamic and alive. Sometimes I get a little annoyed when we talk about old-fashioned religion. Old-fashioned compared to what? Where does that go? There is nothing old-fashioned about Christ. He has always been. He always will be. He is living and dynamic, and we cannot afford to forget about what saves. A spirit of godliness saves. Responding in the way of Christ no matter what happens around or to us *saves*.

It Isn't Easy

Incorporating the sin-breaking characteristics of self-control, perseverance, and godliness is no simple process. The character God desires to develop in us will not happen until we take who we are and, in a no-holds-barred decision, give Him everything.

For this very reason, make every effort to add to your faith goodness; and to goodness, knowledge; and to knowledge, self-control; and to self-control, perseverance; and to perseverance, godliness....

—2 Peter 1:5–6

God longs to give you *immeasurably more*, but first you must give Him all of you.

WORKBOOK

Chapter Three Questions

Question: When it comes to aiming for self-control in your life, are you more focused on what you *shouldn't* do or what you *should* do? Do you feel that focusing on the things you shouldn't do helps you to keep from doing them, or does it give them more attention and weight in your life? What are some things you *should* do on which you need to focus your attention? Do you think that focusing on the "shoulds" makes it easier or harder to walk with self-control? Why?

_____

_____

_____

_____

Question: *Human endurance labors under the "why" of the moment. Godly perseverance dwells in the wealth of God's grace.* When you find yourself in trying times, do you get lost in the "why" of what you are going through? How does that detract from perseverance? How will focusing on the wealth of God's grace help you to walk with perseverance?

_____

_____

_____

_____

_____

_____

_____

_____

_____

_____

_____

Question: What do your life and behavior look like when you go through a crisis? Do you continue to spill over with love, service, and evangelism? Do you spread joy even in the midst of your own sorrow? Is your life still Kingdom-focused, or do you become self-engrossed and focused on doing what you think will make you feel better? What do you think will make you the kind of person who exudes godliness even in crisis?

_____

_____

_____

_____

_____

_____

_____

_____

_____

_____

_____

Action: How are you actively effecting change to bring self-control, perseverance, and godliness to the forefront of your life? Are you asking God daily to shape you? Are you doing the hard work of addressing the problem areas in your life? Make a plan and a commitment to spend time with God daily to address these things in your life.

Chapter Three Notes

CHAPTER FOUR

Cultivating Godly Relationships

At the beginning of our marriage, Queenie got really sick. She was struggling with a fever, and I decided that I would fix it. I would take care of her. I did everything I could do to make things right and help her to feel better. Suddenly she screamed, "Get out of here!"

"What?! How can she possibly want me to leave? I'm nursing her back to health!" I couldn't believe it.

The problem was that I was giving her what I *thought* she needed, but what she really needed was to be left alone. That was hard for me to accept. When I am sick, I want to be babied. I want to be smothered with affection. I felt like I was not being a good husband if I did not give her that very same treatment.

Our tendency to focus on ourselves and our own wants and desires can cloud our relationships with others—and our relationship with God. When we talk about love, we tend to be selfish in our perceptions of it. In relationships, people often say, "If you loved me, you would...," or, "If you loved me, you wouldn't...." If you think about it, such expressions define love purely in terms of selfish desire. It's only what *we* want that matters.

However, Jesus died on the cross *with us in mind*. He

gave us what we needed, not what He wanted or needed. Think about that: the holy God, pure and blameless in every respect, sacrificed Himself for our sins. I would think that God would want nothing to do with a creation that curses Him, ignores Him, uses His name as an exclamation point, and finds innumerable ways to alter the truth He has revealed to us. I would think that at some point, He would stop putting up with us, yet He continues to extend His forgiveness and grace when we need it. That is a demonstration of love.

> *For this very reason, make every effort to add to your faith goodness; and to goodness, knowledge; and to knowledge, self-control; and to self-control, perseverance; and to perseverance, godliness; and to godliness, mutual affection; and to mutual affection, love.*
> **—2 Peter 1:5–7**

These building blocks of character have led us to one of the biggest imperatives of Christianity: love. This is the top of the tower. It's the final block. Pure love for others is the ultimate goal.

Brotherly Love

What is love? Love is an exercise of the will that grows out of a commitment of the heart. It is more than emotions; it is a decision to embrace someone else regardless of his or her actions. Love is the person of Christ coming alive in us and through us as demonstrated in how we behave in relationships and interact with other people.

*Love is extending ourselves to others
with great vulnerability.*

Remember the sequence upon which we are building. There is the foundation of faith, followed by the block of goodness, which is moral power and zeal. Zeal is not enough, so we add knowledge. This gives zeal some direction. With knowledge, we need self-control, the ability to keep our hands on the wheel while we are going forward. To self-control, we must add perseverance, the ability to stay the course and keep forging ahead. When things seem dark, perseverance enables us to see the light. To perseverance, we add godliness. When we hit godliness, everything shifts from inner change to outward change because godliness cannot exist independent of relationships. To godliness, we are to add brotherly kindness. The Greek word used here is *philadelphia*.[17]

I am a native Pennsylvanian, and I have spent some time visiting Philadelphia, the City of Brotherly Love. Great title, great label, but I am not sure that it lives up to its claim. I am sad to say that there are also a lot of churches where you will not find brotherly love. When you walk in, instead of feeling welcomed, loved, and accepted, you immediately feel like an outsider.

I will never forget the day Queenie and I walked into a church we were visiting and sat down. I was sitting there, looking forward to a great service, when suddenly a man walked up beside me and stuck out his hand. I thought, *"Great! I'm being welcomed!"* Then he said, "You'll have to excuse us, but you're in our seat."

My mind flooded with responses: *"Why is this his seat? Did he buy it? Is his name on it?"* I kept my thoughts to myself, but you can probably imagine how we felt in that moment. Do you think that we were inclined to return? No way! In that moment, I knew that it would be both our first and our last visit.

You show brotherly kindness when you extend your arms and your heart to another. There is a warmth about you that is inviting to anybody you meet, whether in the church or outside of it.

Epictetus, a Stoic philosopher, was not only stoic, but also arrogant. He felt that he should remain single because he did not have time to be bothered with little snotty-nosed kids. A quote from him: "How can he who has to teach mankind run to get something in which to heat the water to give the baby his bath?"[18] What a warm, friendly, wonderful man he was. Good grief!

There is something deeply wrong with any person or religion that finds the demands of human relationships to be a nuisance.[19] We sometimes see this same self-centered distancing in the church. It's not social distancing or spiritual distancing; it's a skewed focus and distorted priorities. It is sad when people who claim to love Christ find normal human relationships to be a pain that demands too much of them.

Life as a Recluse

Nowadays people can become extremely reclusive. We come home from work and go into our houses, where we have our big TVs. We close the doors, and it's nice and comfortable in there. We whip up some popcorn and sit in front of an alternate world created by people who probably have nothing to do with God. There is no fellowship, no brotherly love, being given and received.

Someone calls, and we glance at the caller ID to sort out whom we will talk to and whom we will ignore. Even when it's someone we like, we let the call go to voicemail. We set people aside and turn on Netflix instead.

Churches do this, too. Instead of having a desire to get out and meet people where they are, we want everything to take place within the four walls of the building. We think that witnessing is inviting someone to Sunday morning service, and we carefully plan every event so that people will come to us. We glitz up our worship services with lights, smoke machines, and scintillating graphics. We make church a destination or an experience when it should be a fellowship of brotherly love that is not confined to the church building. Lights, loud music, and in-church activities will not necessarily help the person whose life is going up in smoke or the person who has sworn off churchgoing completely.

When COVID-19 hit, the church came face to face with a startling reality. She had become so focused on gathering that she had neglected going. The church had to scramble to get the gospel out in a new way. She had to learn how to build loving relationships in a no-contact environment. What a challenge!

There was a church that was not growing, and over time, it started to fall into disrepair. The parking lot was the first thing that needed attention, but it was going to cost a lot of money. As the leaders of the church were discussing the issue, one of them said, "Listen, if people really want to be here, they can park on the street or find a spot!"

What? He completely missed the fact that many people *don't* want to be in church. Unchurched people are not sitting in their homes, thinking, *"Boy, I can't wait to get to church! I hope it's no hassle to find parking!"* No way! They are thinking about all the reasons they shouldn't go, and they are looking for any excuse to drive away without entering the church building.

If we think that people are clamoring for what we have, then we are missing the point of brotherly love. It's about sacrificing our selfish desires so we can lead people into the presence of God.

What We Protect

In one of the churches I pastored, there was a married couple really fired up about reaching people who did not know Jesus. They started bringing kids to our Wednesday night children's program. Soon the couple came to me and asked, "Hey, can we use the church van?" Their car was packed, and they needed the space to accommodate more kids. Soon after that, they asked to use the church bus. Before I realized it, this couple was bringing forty-five kids every Wednesday night.

"This is great!" I thought, but not everyone shared my excitement.

One family in the church approached me and said, "We've got all these kids running around the church with no parents!"

At first, I thought that they were saying it in a positive way. I thought they were so excited about the kids that they wanted to find a way to reach the parents, so I initially responded, "Isn't that great?"

Apparently, it was not. When I said those words, the family realized that they sounded like complainers. They needed to have some justification for their perspective that the kids were a nuisance, so they said, "Well, these kids are running around and spilling Kool-Aid on the carpet."

I looked at them and said, "Well, did Jesus die for the carpet or the kids? Which one should we try to save?" It was one of my bolder moments, but what I said is true. I am convinced that most churches would rather save the carpet. People get upset about the dents in the wall and the liability and the expenses, but they are not upset about people who do not know Christ. Where is our heart to reach out?

In another church I pastored, I wanted to do some renovations. I thought that it would be a good move to take out a wall and make a meeting room bigger, but not everyone agreed. Our board of trustees called a meeting and invited me to attend—which is when a pastor knows that he is in trouble. I met with them, and they were pretty upset. One of the guys was screaming at me. *Screaming!* In another one of my bolder moments, I said to him, "Do you get this upset about people who are lost and dying and going to hell?" He ended up leaving the church over a wall.

I still feel bad about how that transpired, but the fact is that we need to check our brotherly love. Where are our hearts? Are we extending our arms to others? Do our hearts go out to those who are hurting and those who are lost? Are we willing to help them?

We spend way too much time protecting what does not matter. Don't you think that if God decides that the carpet needs to be replaced, He will make a way? He fed the Israelites with manna from heaven and parted the Red Sea so His people could cross. Don't you think that He has the logistics figured out? Even if He does not come through and fix that Kool-Aid spill, don't you think that He has an ultimate plan?

Some of the things that annoy us in a church are the very things that I believe God absolutely savors. We look at a hole in the wall and think about patching, painting, and blending it back in. God looks at that hole and thinks, *"Greg made that hole. Greg needs My love."* Those stains, those holes, those expensive repairs are signs of a church in action. They are part of a much bigger picture, and I tend to think that God is pleased when a church welcomes people and those people leave a mark.

A friend of mine was interviewing for a position in a church. He did not know much about the church going into the interview, but he was surprised by some of the things they said. He told me that they had a rule: he was only to recruit kids for his youth program if their parents were also able to attend. "They told me only to bring children with parents, Tom," he said to me.

Is that brotherly love? Is that the heart of God? If we feel that way, how can we say that the love of God lives in us? See, it's easy to yell our affirmation in church and get excited about telling others about Jesus, but what are we actually doing to make a difference?

Is your church exploding? Are you out there gathering everyone you can get? Are you going to where they are? What are you doing to say, "Lord, I'm not going to be reclusive. I'm not going to hide"?

Out of the reclusive mindset comes a system in which churches only function for themselves. Somebody says, "Hey, let's start a singles ministry." Somebody else says, "But we don't have any singles, so what do we need that for?"

Another says, "Let's expand our nursery!" Someone responds, "Why? We only have two babies in the church body."

The mentality is that we should plan for what we have and no more. What does this communicate to the different types of people who may walk through the door? It says, "We don't want to grow. We don't have a vision for the future. We're not making room for God to do something in our midst." In other words, "We're fine the way we are. We don't need you."

The Nature of Sin

When we stay reclusive and in our comfort zone, withholding our brotherly love, not only do we resist meaningful change, but we also lose our heart for the lost. If we think that the spiritual heat in a church service needs ramping up, we hope that the pastor rises to the occasion.

We hope that he beats us up with his sermon. We want fire and brimstone to rain down. We hope that the saved become *more* saved, but we do not possess the love that would compel us to go out and reach the lost.

I wish that I could tell you this with laughter, but Christians act in despicable ways in the church. They fight over sound, the temperature of the building, music volume, and a quiver full of other issues upon which they put sharp points before shooting their arrows.

Instead, we need to reflect in our behavior what it means to be filled with the Spirit of God and His love. There should be something distinct about us that is so compelling that it brings others to a point of hungering for what we have. That is our mission, but we have forgotten about our mission. We have even forgotten that we have been cleansed.

Second Peter 1:8–9 reads:

> For if you possess these qualities in increasing measure, they will keep you from being ineffective and unproductive in your knowledge of our Lord Jesus Christ. But whoever does not have them is nearsighted and blind, forgetting that they have been cleansed from their past sins.

As a kid, I used to wonder, *"How could I be born into sin? What terrible thing could I possibly have done before I was born? Did I kick too hard in the womb? Did I tie my mother's umbilical cord into knots? What did I do?"* Being born into sin means that sinning comes naturally to us. Doing wrong is part of who we are. It's why parents discipline their children. It's why we have police officers. It's why we have prisons. It's not natural for people to do what is right, and that's the reality. We are not innately good.

Then Jesus Christ came. He died on the cross, and He sent His Holy Spirit. On one hand, we have an innately sinful nature, but on the other hand, we have a path toward righteousness. God desires to give us a new nature so that instead of sitting in our sin and accepting it, we can become transformed. We can become filled with the Spirit and move forward on the path of righteousness.

Over time, if this is you, you will find that it becomes more natural to do what is right. That does not mean that you no longer do wrong, but rather that you are more inclined to do right as you lean on Jesus and chase righteousness. When we allow Jesus to live in us and we bring these qualities from 2 Peter into our lives, His love becomes the natural response we have to those around us.

Think about how different that is from so much of what we see in the church today. We see ungodly biting and caustic attitudes toward the lost. That is not what God intends! He intends for us to respond to people with His loving heart.

Call to Action

To change the body of Christ in this direction, we need to encourage the body of Christ. We need to learn to *compliment* each other with words as we see evidence of these building blocks in people's lives. This means complimenting the Sunday school teacher, the nursery volunteer, the people who are pouring godly values into your children. It means thanking those who listen to us when we are down and acknowledging the work that the pastor puts in every single day.

We also need to *complement* each other in service. That means we complete one another and work together as the body of Christ should. If you see an area in which I am weak, I don't need you to get up and say, "Wow, you're a loser in that area, Tom!" Rather, I need you to say, "I see an area where I can help you. I want to come alongside you in this."

When we come together, we are stronger. Where one is weak, another is strong. Our skills, talents, and gifts can work together in beautiful unity. This means coming alongside your brother or sister in Christ and stepping in where he or she may be lacking. This has nothing to do with nitpicking weaknesses in others or feeling superior or having a savior complex. It's about seeing a need, knowing whether you can help, and then rising to the occasion.

When you see areas in the church that need help and you sit back and say to your friend, "I could fix that," well, go fix it! Do you think that if you offer your help and expertise, you are going to be turned down? No way!

When you have a gift that will add to the health and life of the church in a positive way, exercise it. When you see others trying to operate in areas where they are not gifted, do not criticize them. Rise up, offer to take over, and allow them to move to a position of their own giftedness. Let them be unleashed in the areas where they have strengths.

We also need to learn to listen to one another. I fully believe that we are not good listeners because listening means that we have to assume some responsibility. It brings us into the problem. It makes us accountable. It forces us to get involved in someone else's life.

Someone once told me that they were emotionally expensive. What powerful words! This person was right; they required more care than most. One of the reasons we resist being good listeners is that we know there is a cost. All too often, instead of listening, as soon as we say hello, we are looking for an opportunity to say goodbye. We are looking for a way out of the conversation because we do not want to get involved in anyone else's mess. Instead, we need to pray that God would give us a burden for people who are hurting, those who need love, and those who do not know Jesus.

I remember when I was a youth pastor in the mid-seventies. Things were a lot different back then. We went door to door in evangelism, and it wasn't so bad. Of course, nowadays that is the least effective way to evangelize. To be honest, I am not sure that we had lasting results back then, but we pretended like we did.

One particular time, it was winter in Indiana. It was cold and snowy. We were going door to door, and I was freezing. My nose was every color but the right one!

Have you ever gone up to a house in the cold and dark? A resident would open the door, and light and warmth would rush over us. We would lean forward and think, *"I want to be in there."*

It just so happened that on this bitterly cold night, we were out making calls on mostly Christians. I had about three youth-group kids with me, and we went up to those homes shivering and shaking. The doors would open, and we would feel the warmth from the homes. We would tell them who we were, and they would respond, "Oh, we attend such and such church and are believers. It's so nice what you are doing. We hope things go well for you." Then the doors would slam shut.

It went on like this for about an hour. Finally, we went to a home, and the door opened. The light and warmth washed over us, and I started to talk. By now, my words were confused and jumbled. Before I could get out much more than a "hello," the lady said, "Come in!" The kids bulldozed by me as I tried to respond to her, and she said, "Don't say anything. Let me fix you some hot chocolate and cookies." I remember thinking, *"Was that door pearly? Did we just enter heaven?"*

We went inside and sat down. She came out of the kitchen about ten minutes later and passed out hot chocolate and cookies. My speech was starting to return to normal, and I said, "Ma'am, let me tell you why we're here."

She said, "Stop, before you say anything, I want to tell you that I'm a (she named a religious sect), and I want to tell you about my faith."

Guess what the kids talked about on our way back that night. They talked about how we had been turned away at all of the Christian homes, but the woman from a different religious sect invited us in. "Why is that, Pastor Tom?" they asked. I did not have an answer for that one.

You see, talking about brotherly kindness and extending it are two different things. I could speculate about why the Christians did not invite us into their homes. I don't think that they didn't like us. I don't think that they were mean or cruel. They just did not want to be bothered. They did not want a kink in their routine or their plans. We would have interrupted their evening. That mindset is not brotherly kindness or love.

Agape Love and Forgiveness

Second Peter 1:7 takes this truth one step further:

...and to mutual affection, love.

This is *agape* love,[20] the highest form of love. It's the kind of love that was given not just when we were sweet and wonderful, but even when we were committing adultery, when we were taking the Lord's name in vain, when we were lying through our teeth, when we were doing everything despicable in the sight of God.

But God demonstrates his own love for us in this: While we were still sinners, Christ died for us.
—Romans 5:8

This is the no-holds-barred love. It's the kind of love that says, "What you do isn't the issue. How I give to you has nothing to do with what pleases me at the moment. I give because it is what you need."

Agape love is a love you give by choice,
and as a result, it becomes a choice love.
It is something sacred.

What does it mean to extend agape love? It means that you are giving the same unconditional love and acceptance that God has given you. There is nothing you can do to earn it except to breathe. That's it. I am going to love you, period. To the best of my ability, I am going to extend understanding. There will be no condemnation. It's not my job to condemn you or to judge you, but to keep pointing you to Christ. Agape love means that when you harm me, there will be forgiveness.

I am confident that one hundred percent of us have been hurt at some point or another in our lives. If you are like me, if you could peel back your skin and expose your heart, there would be all kinds of scars from relationships in which you were rejected and hurt and from times when people said hurtful things to or about you. There have been times when you gave what you felt was your very best in a relationship, and you got slapped in the face. Those scars remain. They create a map of insecurity and pain, but agape love breaks through all of that.

I am not writing as someone who walks flawlessly through the challenges of life. I know the agonies of failing in many professional endeavors, of fighting to get the bills paid, of being unfaithful in spite of the vows I spoke, of hurting people when that was the last thing on earth I ever wanted to do, of dreaming dreams that were never realized, and of falling short of the standard I wanted to meet. I get it. There is no halo over my head. No one is trumpeting my life as a stellar example of perfection. However, I have learned a lot, and I can say that I am learning what it means to navigate life in the presence of God. I am not speaking as a theologian; I am speaking as a common man living in an upside-down world with a God who knows the right turns to take in life. Through Christ, I have experienced and learned about forgiveness.

It was Jesus who said, "Forgive them." Forgive the people who have hurt you the most. We do not like that solution. Forgiveness lets the other person off free while we are stuck with the wounds, but here is the reality of it: we all get off free.

I can give you more reasons than I can count why I have no business opening the Word of God to you. I can give you all kinds of reasons why God could have looked at me and said, "Tom, you've got to be kidding Me. You want Me to forgive you?"

I remember the day as if it just happened. The emotions are still fresh, as if they were just picked off a tree of angst and placed in a boiling pot of regret. I know what it's like to sin and hurt people I love. I hurt my wife deeply. Confessing the despicable sins I committed to the woman I love was one of the most devastating times of my life. The pain it brought to both of us was unimaginable unless you have been through it. My words were like knives, each penetrating to the deepest recesses of her heart. It was painful and numbing all at the same time.

"How could this be?" she thought. *"How could this man I trusted do this to me? How could I have not seen it?"* This and a myriad of other questions raced through her mind as she sought to catch her balance and make sense out of senseless behavior. However, out of her pool of emotional blood, she responded with love and grace.

Instead of throwing me out like spoiled refuse, she stood by me and committed to working through the issues. Her response was overpowering.

Don't misunderstand me—it's not that she was not angry, stunned, crushed, or empty. She was all of that and more. However, she was also a woman willing to look at the bigger picture and do what it took to fight for our marriage. I am deeply in love with this lady, and surprisingly to some, she is still in love with me. That did not mean the road back would be a cakewalk. There were many tense and anger-filled moments in our home.

Words that had their origin in a bloodbath of betrayal and were stuffed with a maze of confused emotions would emerge and spill out, not because she wanted to hurt me, although I suspect that at times she did, but because she wanted to understand something that was never on her radar, something that she never thought would enter her personal life. I had hurt her at the deepest level. Was there any hope for recovery? Would it be possible to find our way out of this maze of pain and betrayal? The answer is a resounding "yes!" When Christ is the one to whom we turn, there is always hope. As you can see, I have a big list of reasons why I shouldn't be forgiven. Even so, I got off scot-free. I was forgiven, restored, and set free!

Let me give you a simple definition for forgiveness.

Forgiveness is when you assume the consequences of someone else's wrong.

That's forgiveness. It's not a warm, fuzzy feeling. It does not mean that you are overwhelmed with emotion or that the pain of what happened does not bother you ever again. It just means that you value that person more than his or her wrongdoing. It means that you are fully exercising these building blocks of character that we have been discussing.

Jesus Christ assumed the consequences for our sin. He paid the price for our sin. The only way we can forgive others is to do the same, to assume the consequences for their sin.

I have had to learn a lot about forgiveness through the years, but I think that the most profound lesson happened when our family was getting ready to move from Indiana to work in South Carolina. Our daughter, whom we call Punk, had just completed her freshman year in college, and she was staying on there for her sophomore year.

It was a Saturday, and we were going to leave on Sunday afternoon. Everything was packed in the truck, ready for departure. Queenie and I were staying at my parents' house, preparing to leave the next day. Queenie and Punk went out for a drive that Saturday afternoon, and I happened to be standing at the front door when I saw them pull into our driveway. When they pulled in, I looked out and saw that Queenie had a heavy look on her face. She motioned for me to come out to the car.

I remember jumping into the back seat of the car. Queenie was in the driver's seat, and Punk was sitting up front as well. That's when I learned that two weeks prior to that, our daughter had been raped.

At that moment, there was nothing holy going through my mind. If I had my desires as a human being, I would have left immediately to find that guy. I wanted to make him suffer. I wanted him to hurt like Punk hurt, like I hurt.

That's how I felt humanly. As those feelings were swelling and swimming around inside of me, God immediately started to work on me. I have to tell you that I did not appreciate it. Sometimes when you feel justified in your emotions, you just want the freedom to express yourself, but God began to deal with me. I vividly remember feeling Him ask me, "Tom, do you want her to hold on to this?"

"No, I don't want my little girl to hold on to this!"

"Then you can't hold on to it, either."

In the process of dealing with forgiving this guy, I remembered back in my pastoral career. I've had to handle a lot of sexual abuse trauma in counseling. I remembered talking with a particular lady who had suffered horribly at the hands of her father.

As she was telling me the story, I was sitting there without changing the expression on my face, but inside I wanted to find her father and beat him senseless. That's how I felt as a human being. Again, as vividly as you can possibly imagine, it was almost as if God tapped me on the shoulder in that moment and said, "Tom, the guy you're thinking about, that father—I died for him."

It's one thing to know that Jesus died for everyone, but it's another to deal with the reality of this in moments when you do not feel that a certain person is worthy of being died for. I have forgiven the man who violated my daughter, but please understand that I do not say that out of a sense of holiness or righteousness. I share it as a testimony of what God can do. If we are willing to forgive, God gives us the grace and the ability to do it.

If you are holding on to any unforgiveness, do not blame God. Do not blame the circumstances. Do not act like your injustice was too much. What you are doing is valuing your sin or someone else's sin more than you value a holy, clean relationship with God.

I was an active child, but my son, Augie, was active beyond belief. I can only imagine that as I was growing up, my parents routinely prayed, "Lord, give Tom a child just like him!" And boy, did God deliver! Augie was feisty and had an iron will. When he was just a little over two years old, Queenie and I made a horrible mistake: one night, we allowed him to watch *The Incredible Hulk*.

The next Sunday, he went to church and sat in those kid chairs that are just the right size for toddlers. Halfway through class, he stood up, growled like the Hulk, picked up his chair, and threw it across the Sunday school classroom! Imagine the joy of the teacher.

From that point on, it was a weekly occurrence that our son was brought to us every Sunday for being a disturbance. Eventually, the church workers' countenances changed. They went from "Your son is having trouble in class" to "You must be a lousy parent! This has been going on for weeks and weeks!" We were doing everything we knew to do, but Augie had a mind of his own.

When Augie was in the fourth grade, he got a brand-new teacher in Sunday school. The teacher was new to the whole system and did not have knowledge of our son's prior behavior. He had not heard the rumors. I sat Augie down and said, "You get a fresh start here. Let's make the most of it!"

He went to class, and I went about my church responsibilities. Halfway through Sunday school, the new teacher, Richard, walked through the door with Augie on his arm. He sat Augie next to me, and Augie was crying because he knew that he had blown it.

We took him home and administered a little justice. That afternoon, we were sitting around the dinner table when the doorbell rang. It was Richard, Augie's Sunday school teacher. He said, "Can Augie come out and play? I have a kite, and I'd love for him to come out and fly it with me."

That's what he said, but here is what I heard: "Your son has value. I don't care what he did in my class. I love your son."

For this very reason, make every effort to add to your faith goodness; and to goodness, knowledge; and to knowledge,

> *self-control; and to self-control, perseverance; and to per-*
> *severance, godliness; and to godliness, mutual affection;*
> *and to mutual affection, love. For if you possess these qual-*
> *ities in increasing measure, they will keep you from being*
> *ineffective and unproductive in your knowledge of our*
> *Lord Jesus Christ.*
>
> *—2 Peter 1:5–8*

Agape love is believing in people and loving them even when it's tough. Think about what would happen if we were to treat all the kids in our children's ministries this way? How many desperately need someone like Richard to show up and fly a kite with them? How many need to hear that they are valued and loved even when they act out?

When we start expressing to one another that people have value, that families have value, no matter what, it creates big change. It shows others—and us—the immeasurably more. It lets us know that there is *more* to life.

Chapter Four Questions

Question: Is your life characterized by brotherly kindness, or are you more reclusive? How can you endeavor to show more brotherly kindness to others? Are you extending your arms to others? Does your heart go out to those who are hurting and those who are lost? Are you willing to help them?

_____

_____

_____

_____

_____

_____

_____

_____

_____

_____

Question: Do you find yourself complaining about the way things are (or the way they are not) in your church and services? Do you criticize others in the church body for not doing things the way you want or like? Are you an active participant in making your church community all that it can be and that you want it to be? What are your gifts and talents? How can you use them to serve your church?

_____

_____

_____

_____

_____

_____

_____

_____

_____

_____

_____

Question: What does it mean to extend agape love? Is your life characterized by agape love? What are some examples of agape love that you have received and have given? When was the last time you experienced an extension of agape love? When was the last time you extended agape love? What steps can you take to live a life that is more characterized by agape love?

Action: If you are holding on to any unforgiveness, you have a gracious Father who is willing to give you the ability to forgive. With God's help, make a list of people and offenses you are holding on to. Be personal and specific. No matter how long it takes, work through that list with God and surrender your anger, pain, and unforgiveness. Make the choice to forgive and allow the Holy Spirit to help you do it.

Chapter Four Notes

CHAPTER FIVE

Going Deeper:
The Practice of Submission

Second Peter 1:5–7 lays a solid foundation for building up your life in Christ. The building blocks outlined in those verses bring out characteristics that keep us centered in Jesus and moving into the immeasurably more, but this process is not a one-and-done thing. We never graduate from the gospel. In the second half of this book, we are going to look at how to go deeper with these characteristics of faith.

Ephesians 3:14–21 is a passage brimming with a sense of holiness that sweeps over the atmosphere of our entire existence. We must approach this passage honestly and openly. We are standing on holy ground.

For this reason I kneel before the Father, from whom every family in heaven and on earth derives its name. I pray that out of his glorious riches he may strengthen you with power through his Spirit in your inner being, so that Christ may dwell in your hearts through faith. And I pray that you, being rooted and established in love, may have power, together with all the Lord's holy people, to grasp how wide and long and high and deep is the love of Christ, and to know this love that surpasses knowledge—that you may be filled to the measure of all the fullness of God.

Now to him who is able to do immeasurably more than all we ask or imagine, according to his power that is at work within us, to him be glory in the church and in Christ Jesus throughout all generations, for ever and ever! Amen.
                                                                —Ephesians 3:14–21

This passage shows the profound intimacy between a sovereign God and an itinerant servant, the Apostle Paul. It offers a glimpse into the expanse of a burning heart, and it is designed to make us more tempered and refined, more sensitive and holy, more fertile in our receptivity to the truth. These things will not happen miraculously. There must be a deliberate effort on our part to seek and know God.

Paul, the author of the passage, is a great example of this. He showed us what it is to stay in the presence of God and never to leave the side of the Lord. He wrote under the inspiration of the Holy Spirit, yet he demonstrated poised humility. He recognized his place as a humble servant of God, forgiven from his sins and set apart, but he also understood his unique role as an apostle of the gospel of Jesus Christ. He was on the edge of his seat in terms of his expectancy to learn and his readiness to serve.

That is exactly the same posture we need to assume in our spiritual journey: expectancy and readiness in our learning and serving. Only in this position can we grow in our building blocks of character and realize all that God has for us.

Paul's Practice of Submission Was Built on His Recognition of God's Holiness

...I kneel before the Father....

—Ephesians 3:14

Paul's submission to God did not come out of nowhere. In order to submit to God, we have to be humbled. In order to be humbled, we must have a fear and reverence for God. We must recognize the holiness of God, or we will fail to respond in a manner that is humble and submissive.

What happens when we lose a sense of the holy? I will tell you what happens: we begin a downward spiral. Our relationship with God becomes less important, and the re-pugnance of sin becomes less pronounced. When this happens, there is a tendency to grade sin on a scale of 1 to 10, thinking that if we keep our sins on the lower end of the scale, we are in good shape.

Such thinking diminishes the holiness of God. Every sin, large or small, is abhorrent to Him. It's like drinking a glass of water with a speck of dirt in it. We would quickly send it back! How can we think that the smaller sins are not a problem to God?

God is perfect and flawless. Our sins grieve Him. When we forget this, we forget His holiness. When we forget His holiness, we sin more. It's an endless cycle that leads to destruction.

Another thing that happens when we lose a sense of the holiness of God is that life becomes less sacred. The sa-cred is swallowed by the secular, rather than the secular being swallowed by the sacred. We differentiate between the sacred and the secular and begin to isolate our walk with God from our daily living. God becomes a Sunday thought, not an everyday walk.

When we distance ourselves from the holiness of God, He becomes the image of religion rather than the embodiment of life and creation. He represents rules and standards and confinement rather than relationship, safety, and freedom. We become more concerned with our image than God's image, so we shape Him according to our whims and desires. For example, our worship becomes self-gratifying rather than Christ-exalting. We focus on what we like rather than what pleases God.

What we sing becomes more important than to whom we sing.

The further we remove ourselves from the holiness of God, the less important truth becomes. Our opinions become "truth," and what God says becomes secondary. When we speak, we say whatever will make us acceptable to the culture around us, even if what we say is contrary to the truth of God's Word. Cultural values take a higher priority than spiritual values.

Our distance from the holiness of God causes us to lose sight of who the church is supposed to be. She becomes more economically driven than spiritually driven. Church board members ask, "How much does it cost?" instead of "Is it God's will?" They focus on the number in the bank and the resources they have rather than God's desires and His resources. This becomes the standard, regardless of what God desires.

We cannot continue putting God in the back seat and acting like it will have no effect on our lives. In order to recapture a sense of the holy and learn to submit to God the Father, we must take some important steps.

Submission Is Giving Up Control

For this reason I kneel before the Father, from whom every family in heaven and on earth derives its name.
—Ephesians 3:14–15

In the verses leading up to this passage, Paul wrote about profound truths that God revealed to him about the church and, even greater, the Lord Himself. Paul testified that he knew what it was to be saved, to be brought out of a life of sin and transformed into a servant of the Most High God. This was the background leading into this text in which Paul made it clear that he wanted every believer to enter into the type of knowledge and relationship with God that he had. He wanted people to *know God.*

The word *kneel* in this passage indicates more of a bow.[21] Bowing carries with it a significant meaning. When Jews would pray, they would do so standing, arms outstretched. Paul gave a sense in this passage that he was prostrate on the ground, flat-out submitted to God. His introductory words indicate that his prayer was a prayer of intensity, agony, and humility.

Paul had positioned himself humbly, not only physically but also spiritually. He wanted to be humbled spiritually so as to be the most effective servant he could be for Christ. He was not seeking to find the most strategic spot where he could control, escape, defend, or dominate. No, he was, with trust, bowing before the Lord and humbling himself as a servant of the Most High God.

Don't miss what may seem unremarkable to us but was not to Paul: the fact that Paul bowed before the Father. In the Old Testament, God the Father was unapproachable. In the New Testament, Christ came and opened the door to God the Father. The opening of this prayer accentuates a deep humility on the part of Paul, an intimacy between

God and humanity, and a vulnerability on God's part to us. It brings together the unity of all the saints, both in heaven and on earth—unity that exists as a result of the work of Christ.

I have had people tell me that there are a variety of ways I could improve my prayer life: speaking in tongues, raising my arms, lying on the floor, kneeling on the floor, holding hands. Honestly, not one of these things will work. It was not Paul's physical position that made the difference; it was his heart.

Humble submission is desperately needed in the church and the world today. We have become so arrogant that we have begun to undermine the power of God. It's not the position of our bodies that makes a difference; it's the position of our hearts.

Many of us feel self-sufficient. We determine that we will make our own way in life, solve our own problems, create our own opportunities, and heal our own hurts. We become so purposefully independent that we rebel at the thought of becoming dependent on anyone or anything.

That is one of the reasons why so many marriages struggle. One or both partners enter a mutual union with the idea that they will remain independent, not become interdependent. They vie for control, which only leads to a crumbling marriage. Marriage was never meant to be an independent venture. It is, as God's Word says, two becoming one (Genesis 2:24).

There has been an emphasis in the Christian realm that has been greatly abused and has hindered the real significance of spiritual submission and humility. It comes under the heading of spiritual authority. I hear a great deal about the authority of the believer and how he needs to stand up and take charge of what is his.

Now, there is some truth to the idea that many Christians live far below the gifts and graces God has given us, but there has been great abuse in this area, too. I see many who feel very comfortable with giving God orders: "I command the angels to..." or "I command You, Lord, to remove this problem." I remember seeing a sign that read, "When you pray, don't give God orders; report for duty." What a great truth to practice! What's happening is that the saints are misunderstanding their authority. Our authority is over the devil and his forces, not over God, and our authority is good only as long as we are surrendered to the King of kings.

It was November of 1988, and Queenie and I found ourselves in a most unusual situation: we were alone. So, we went out to dinner and a date. After dinner, we were driving around, and I suggested that we add some spark to our lives and go "parking" somewhere. She was a little hesitant, but she was also the passenger. I took her west of town to a new construction site. I parked in front of a house under construction, off the side of the road with my parking lights on, and turned to the love of my life.

We were talking, and Queenie was worried that someone would walk up behind us. I assured her that would not be a problem. But sure enough, a car pulled up behind us with lights flashing, and a sheriff's deputy came to my window. He shined his extra-bright light into my eyes and began a series of gruff interrogating questions.

I thought, *"Should I tell him who I am? Should I tell him that this is my wife? Should I tell him that I'm a pastor? Should I tell him to get lost?"*

Then he said, "Why do you have a baseball bat in your back seat?"

Now, let me be honest. I was starting to get a little miffed. Here I was, a minister of the gospel, and I was being reflected on as if I were a thief, out with another woman! Still, I knew that the officer was only doing his job. It just so happened that there had been several burglaries in the area, and he was being diligent in his duties.

Isn't that often the case with us? God does His part, or another saint is busy following his or her calling for the Kingdom, and we get miffed. Suddenly, we are not the ones in control, and we lash out. We want to hold the reins. When situations in life are of such a nature that we cannot control them in our human strength, we become desperate.

Please listen to a basic truth about walking with Christ and the reality of life:

> *If Christ is not in control of our lives,*
> *we are out of control.*

Those who refuse to surrender and humble themselves before Christ are victims of the very thing they want to avoid: life out of control. When Christ is in control, we can have confidence in life. In this passage, the Greek word Paul used for *Father* is *pater*. It implies a creator, preserver, guardian, and protector.[22] A sense of assured safety and loving care is built into the word. When Paul wrote that he bowed before the Father, he was expressing confidence in God, the object of his worship.

I once received a card from a friend of mine in South Africa. On the front of the card was a picture of three zebras and two impalas drinking from a pond. All five of the animals had their tongues lapping the water, but their eyes were darting all around, on the lookout for predators.

Too often, I think that we are afraid to submit to the Lord for fear that He will prey on us or do some terrible things to us. We view Him as a disciplinarian more than a loving protector. Such a truth points out the next step toward submission.

Submission Is Learning to Trust

Oftentimes a lack of submission reveals not only a desire to control, but also a lack of trust on our part. Trust is not something that comes on a silver platter. We earn it by proving to be trustworthy. We do that by keeping our word, following through with our responsibilities, and developing a holy character. Interestingly enough, God has done *all* of these things! It should be enough to earn our trust and then some, yet many find it difficult to trust their heavenly Father automatically.

If you have had a lousy relationship with your earthly father, you may struggle with this. So often, the scars of our lives form barriers between ourselves and the Lord Jesus Christ. It's not that we don't want to trust the Lord; it's that we don't want to trust anyone. Learning to trust, however, is a must for all of us. We must take that risk, a little at a time, and give it to the Lord.

It blows my mind that God chooses to trust us! In spite of our actions and sin and horrible track record, God trusts us. He gave *us* the calling to take His message throughout the world. It's the most important task, and He entrusted it to us! He did this even after His disciples deserted Him on the cross, denied knowing Him, and had a hard time believing that He had risen again.

God trusts us. He trusts you. The least you can do is to take steps to trust Him in return.

Submission Is Accepting Spiritual Identity

In Paul's spiritual identity, he painted for us a broader picture of life. He brought together the saints who had already gone on to heaven and linked them with those remaining on earth. This passage points out that all who accept Christ bear His name. Regardless of where we may be, heaven or earth, we are under His care.

Peter Sellers, the actor famous from the *Pink Panther* movies, played so many parts that it was said he sometimes became confused as to who he was. The story goes that one day a person asked, "Are you Peter Sellers?" "Not today," he answered.[23]

Too often, I think that we attempt to live one life in the church and a different life outside of church. No wonder we have trouble sorting out our identity! Paul, on the other hand, was true to who he was. In this passage, he was clear that he identified with Christ and those who walk with Christ.

When we are growing up, it is a natural thing to flaunt our independence from time to time. We want people to know that we can stand on our own. There are times when kids, teenagers especially, do not want to be seen with their parents. It's not that they dislike Mom and Dad as much as that they want others to think that they are their own person. They are trying to say, "I'm me, and I don't need family in order to have an identity."

This is not the message Paul gave us. Paul clarified that although he was considered to be a great spiritual leader, he was simply a part of an even greater family. He was not so much a leader as he was a child, and he was not ashamed to identify as such. This passage is an appeal for unity in the church against the forces of Satan, and the strength of that unity is found in the presence of Christ.

Today we are in desperate need of unity in our world and in the church. People are dividing across political, racial, and sexual lines. The church sometimes seeks to be more of a political machine than a spiritual haven.

In one powerful sentence, Paul not only drew the heavenly forces together with the earthly saints, but also underscored that we have intimate access to the Father. Every time we enter into prayer, we talk to the One who has been there from the beginning. God knows everyone who has ever been and will ever be.

Although we do not personally know all the great saints of the past, we do not come into the presence of God as outsiders. We come as children, created by His breath and recreated by His blood. This verse stresses that when you surrender to the Lord, He gives you a name so you can find your identity in Christ.

If I were to ask for a picture of you, chances are that you would groan and say, "No way!" You may have a photograph taken by a good photographer, and when you look at the final proofs, you are still likely to be unhappy with what you see. The photos are not good enough, yet the camera is only reflecting what it sees. When you look at those pictures, you are really saying, "The pictures are not flattering enough."

It's difficult to see ourselves as we really are, but that is what submission and humility are all about. We come humbly into the presence of God and discover that He accepts us just as we are, and when we surrender, He transforms us into what we can be in Him. He takes us to the immeasurably more, where we carry His name, His distinction.

As never before, the saints need to practice submission to Christ. We need to give up control of our lives to Christ. We need to learn to trust in Him, and we need to accept spiritual adoption into His family. It is that submission that paves the road to effective prayer. It is the posture of our hearts, submissive and humble, that will determine the power of our prayers.

There Is a Bigger Picture

As Paul bowed before the Father, he was bringing together all the saints in heaven and on earth. This helps us to understand that life takes place in a much bigger picture than what we observe. Our lives can become confined to our circumstances and understanding, so we miss the *more* God offers. When we are pressed down by our hurts and crises, submission becomes fearful rather than helpful. We lose sight of the bigger picture.

When I was in the third grade, living in Elizabeth, Pennsylvania, I went to the other side of town to a small little store that carried a certain kind of candy I liked. I had saved my money, and I was eager to put it to good use. Did I mention that Elizabeth was a town with a large number of gangs and bullies? There was a person we called "Moneys," named for his ability to commandeer money from smaller victims. On this particular trip to the store, I did not encounter Moneys. However, I did come face to face with another well-known bully, an eighth grader more than twice my size whose countenance bore a slight resemblance to Fagin in the original movie version of *Oliver Twist.*[24]

When I arrived at the store, Young Fagin was there to greet me. He sauntered over and said that he wanted a nickel. Brave soul that I was, I responded that I didn't have a nickel. Now, Fagin was no dummy. In fact, he knew where I lived, and it didn't take a rocket scientist to know that I didn't come clear across town to this store just to browse.

With a bit more authority, he said, "Give me a nickel." Again I responded, "I don't have a nickel." It was at that moment when he took matters into his own hands—literally. He grabbed me by the lapels and pulled me close to him. His breath covered my face, forming a cloud of fear as he once again demanded a nickel, and this time he recited the consequences of failing to produce that nickel. He threatened me with bodily harm at the hand of his two weapons of mass destruction: his fists.

There comes a time in life when the bigger picture matters. In the small picture, I had come for candy. In the small picture, a beating by a bully and cheating death never entered my mind when I left home that morning and headed out on this little adventure. The bigger picture, however, revealed that my physical well-being had greater value than the candy.

I looked this wannabe prizefighter in the eye and said authoritatively, "I don't have a nickel." As he drew his fist back to unleash his first assault, I added, "I have a dime!" We walked together into the store, where he had the storeowner give him what he wanted, and I paid with my dime for the five-cent cost of the item. Now, here comes the amazing ending to the story. He let me keep the change, a nickel. Can you believe it? As a thief, he had a target, and when the potential plunder exceeded what he had in mind, well, it didn't matter. He stuck to the nickel. Even in his world of wrong, he failed to see the bigger picture.

Our inability to see the bigger picture will always cost us, but Paul saw it. He understood that he was a part of a bigger family; he was a servant of God. He was ready to bow and listen to whatever God had to say, no matter the cost. It was this bigger picture that drove him, not his circumstances, not his emotions, not his desires or personal expectations.

You see, it was not a set of rules that drove the Apostle Paul; it was a sacred relationship with the King of kings. His life in Christ mattered more than the nickels he could have piled up in his time on earth. The sooner we realize that there is a bigger picture going on and that bigger picture is a surrendered relationship with Jesus Christ, the sooner we will enter into the immeasurably more.

WORKBOOK

Chapter Five Questions

Question: What is sin? How do you perceive the sin in your life? Do you think of all sin as dishonoring to a perfect God, or do you think of sin as measured on a scale of 1 to 10? Is it your tendency to consider the sin you perceive to be on the lower end of the scale as not a big deal to you and your relationship with God? Ask God to show you His heart toward the sin in your life.

_____

_____

_____

_____

_____

_____

_____

_____

_____

Question: Do you value your independence and authority? Do you value those things to the detriment of your relationship with God? Do you find it difficult to submit to His authority and the authority of His Word? If so, why? Is there a part of you that does not trust God? Ask God to show you the root of why you find it difficult to trust and surrender to Him.

_____

_____

_____

_____

_____

_____

_____

_____

_____

_____

_____

Question: *He was ready to bow and listen to whatever God had to say, no matter the cost. It was this bigger picture that drove him, not his circumstances, not his emotions, not his desires or personal expectations.* Are you driven by your circumstances, emotions, or desires? If so, ask God to show you the bigger picture of His purposes in your life and in the world. Write down what He reveals to you.

_____

_____

_____

_____

_____

_____

_____

_____

_____

_____

_____

Action: The time to give up control is now. Set aside some time and write out a prayer of submission in a journal or notebook. Confess in what ways you have gone your own way and chosen independence over submission. Ask God to show you His goodness and trustworthiness. From that place of revelation and connection with God, let submission flow from your heart.

Chapter Five Notes

CHAPTER SIX

Falling into the "Whole" of God

I pray that out of his glorious riches he may strengthen you with power through his Spirit in your inner being, so that Christ may dwell in your hearts through faith. And I pray that you, being rooted and established in love....
—Ephesians 3:16–17

Hey, we all know what it's like to trip over a hole or fall into a hole. Think about this with me: we need to fall into the "whole" of God. We will not experience the immeasurably more if we are only looking for bits and pieces of God. We need to want all of Him just as He wants all of us. This means that we become fully immersed in the fullness of God.

In our culture, people bend over backwards to look good. We exercise, diet, train, run, and buy products that will allegedly help us to look better, but what about the soul? What plan is on the market to help us lose the excess weight and baggage of sin? What exercise regime will build up the muscles and strength of our souls? What drink can we buy that will give all the necessary nutrients for our spirits? What aerobic exercises are there for sagging hope and depressed emotions?

*Those who want only a piece of God
cannot experience the peace of God.*

The world chases feverishly after euphoria, craving to live above the woes of everyday life, and all the while, the church sits idle, thanking God for her padded pews and orderly services. When people come to church, we sometimes are more concerned that they get a bulletin for the service than a burden for the lost.

We want them to like our gathering without checking to see if they love our Lord. We want them to enjoy the music without praying over them that God would heal them of spiritual deafness. We work more diligently to make sure that people are comfortable in the service than convicted by truth.

Don't get me wrong here. We do not possess the ability to convict hearts or inflict genuine guilt. Rather, it is the Holy Spirit who convicts us of our sins (John 16:8). Of course, that does not stop some pastors from browbeating their people and trying to saddle them with guilt over anything that comes to mind. This approach is simply another form of control, as church leaders assume the role of judge instead of trusting the Lord to do His work.

There is no way we can artificially induce a spiritual high and expect to fill our hearts with God's lasting fullness. There is no way we can play with only a part of God and use Him for our own personal gain without coming up empty. You see, Jesus did not die on the cross so you and I could look good or feel good, but rather so we could *be* good. He wants us to know what it means to be complete and productive in Christ. He wants us to experience Him, to fall into the "whole" of Christ, to be completely His.

*I pray that out of his glorious riches he may strengthen you
with power through his Spirit in your inner being, so that
Christ may dwell in your hearts through faith. And I pray
that you, being rooted and established in love....*
—**Ephesians 3:16–17**

Oh, but there is more!

Running with Stamina

One of the problems with believers today is a lack of spiritual stamina. We are spiritually out of shape! When we lack spiritual endurance, we move from a mindset of victory to one of survival.

Ephesians 3:16 reads, "I pray that out of his glorious riches he may strengthen you with power through his Spirit in your inner being." Here the Apostle Paul expressed a longing for believers to have a greater understanding of who God really is. He prayed that we would have strength for this and that we would have what it takes to be fruitful and productive for the Lord.

Specifically, he prayed that we would be strengthened with power. The Greek word used here for *strengthen* is *krataioō*, which means to "increase in vigor" or "empower."[25] Paul was addressing not only strength, but also stamina. We need to have our hearts revived in terms of our zeal for Christ.

One of the challenges we face today is a lack of stamina. Sadly, our zeal for the Lord dies out all too quickly. One of the key reasons is that we are spiritually out of shape. I see this unfolding in a few ways.

This can occur when people come to Christ and get fired up. They are ready to conquer the world. They dive into sharing their faith and serving in every way they can, but at some point along the way, they neglect the importance of being fed. They run full steam ahead without any plan to replenish their energy, and sooner or later, they burn out. That's when they enter survival mode.

Another way I have seen this happen is with people who sit in the church pew week after week. They eat steadily at the table of God, but they do nothing with that spiritual nourishment. They don't exercise their faith! They don't apply to their lives the truth and power they have been given. I think of these as obese believers, wallowing in a tub of information that has never been converted into wisdom or action.

When I am physically out of shape, it's tough to play a sport for any length of time without paying dearly. What's more, when I am tired, I am not nearly as competitive. There is no gas in the tank. My goal becomes survival, not victory.

Spiritually, that's where many of God's children are. They are either running on fumes or inexperienced with putting what they have been given to godly use. They do not know how to keep their walk fresh, and they find themselves simply trying to survive instead of seeing spiritual victory in their lives. This is the focus of Paul's prayer. He longed to see us come alive, get in shape, get fired up, and *do* something with our faith in a way that is responsible and effective.

Have you ever had a furnace or water heater that required a pilot light? When that light goes out, the result is no heat. Paul's plea to be strengthened carries the connotation of reaching into a space that requires a gas pilot light and igniting it. The pilot light comes to life and heats up what is around it. Then, as long as it's not snuffed out or burning too hot, it maintains the proper level of heat and energy output. We need to be strengthened as if we were pilot lights, ignited and on fire.

Tapping into the Supernatural

...with power through his Spirit....
—Ephesians 3:16

...with might through His Spirit....
—Ephesians 3:16 *(NKJV)*

If we are going to be on fire, if we are going to be more than we can be on our own, we must tap into the supernatural power of God, the glorious riches God has supplied for us. These glorious riches, however, are not embodied in the external blessings we receive from the Lord; they are found in the residing presence of the Holy Spirit.

All too often, we look for God's blessings in the form of material possessions. We think that a big house, a nice retirement account, and a high-paying job are indications of God's blessing on our lives. This thinking is shallow and far from God's intent! That is not to say that He won't bless us materially, but His big gift to us, the main thing He wants to give us, is Himself, His presence in our lives. Jesus did not die on the cross to pad my bank account or give me a nice car. Anyone who teaches that kind of cheap gospel is a quack!

In this passage, Paul prayed not only for igniting strength and vigor, but also that we would be strengthened with might, or power. On the surface, it sounds a bit redundant. *Strength* and *might* in the English language carry similar connotations. However, the Greek word *dýnamis* does not speak only of force, strength, and ability; it takes it a few steps beyond.

Dýnamis speaks of a power for performing miracles,[26] the power to carry something into effect, *the ability to do anything.*[27] When Paul prayed for *dýnamis*, he was not asking that we would be strengthened by an ordinary pick-me-up. He was praying for the kind of power that God offers, a supernatural power beyond ourselves.

What do you draw from when all of your human resources are exhausted? Where do you go when you have sought counsel from every person you know but still do not have clarity of direction?

Many people comment that they do not have what it takes to live the Christian life, and they are correct. That's what Paul was praying for: a power beyond ourselves. This kind of might enables our hearts to be ignited and also gives us the ability to be the spark in someone else's life.

I remember sitting at the table with a man desperate to find hope. In front of him were four empty beer bottles, and he was working on a fifth. He was smoking cigarette after cigarette, and cursing and anger flowed from his mouth. *"What can I do?"* were the words running through my mind.

This man wanted Christ, and the Lord lit a flame in his heart that night. He went on to surrender his life to Christ and to become a trusted board member in the church and a mighty prayer warrior. He experienced the power of ignition, and he stayed the course with spiritual stamina provided by the Holy Spirit. This power is available to you and me through Christ.

The Honor of Investing

Paul provided unique insight into the might that God offers, telling us that it comes out of His glorious riches. When we consider someone rich, there are probably a lot of things we would like to receive from that person, such as money, privileges, gifts, or attention.

God's glorious riches bring far different benefits. Perhaps we ask God for a special band of angels to surround us, for an ability to stave off the enemy, for a manifestation of the Spirit, or for special attention and favor. There are many things God has in His storehouse of riches, but none of them is good enough for what He ultimately has in mind for us. Note that Paul wrote about God's "*glorious riches*" (Ephesians 3:16, emphasis added). The word *dóxa* is used in this verse.[28] *Dóxa* is not only what God does, but also who He is, exhibited in any way He reveals Himself.

God's glory cannot be separated from Him. In light of that, Paul's prayer comes alive. This *might* does not come from God's trove of riches, nor is it embodied in a representation of God. The gift Paul wrote about in this passage is the Spirit Himself.

This is where so many saints go wrong. We want what God has, not who He is. We want gifts without the Giver. We want visible signs instead of the Holy Spirit. We want earthly security over spiritual security. We want the Lord to make us comfortable more than we want Him to make us compassionate. We expect Him to give us what we want instead of wanting what He gives. We want to confine ourselves to earthly understanding instead of seeking godly understanding. Out of God's glorious riches come the person and power of the Holy Spirit, and that's where true power and honor lie.

There is a story of a grieving widow who was discussing her late husband with a friend. "My Albert was such a good man, and I miss him so. He provided well for me with that $500,000 insurance policy, but I would give a thousand of it just to have him back."[29]

Is that how we treat God? There are too many of us who are content with God's wealth and ignore who He is. We are willing to sacrifice very little in order to be truly consumed by Him. God wants to invest not only what He has, but also who He is. He wants to give His all.

It's not an angel living in me or some prefabricated

spirit or a psychological personality that I have manufactured. Residing in me is the living, almighty God of the universe. Paul was clear that the Spirit resides in our "inner being" (Ephesians 3:16). The Lord does not desire to ride on the superficial edge of our pursuits. He wants to take up residence in the innermost sanctuary of our being.

Often we talk about the Lord sitting next to us or riding with us or leading us, but He is living *within* us! He knows our every thought. All of the secrets, agonies, fears, goals, and aspirations of our soul become the furniture on which God sits.

Once this clicks, we understand what it means to be strengthened with power through the Spirit in our inner man. God does not want us to have only His gifts and then stop there. That would mean possessing only a part of who He is and what He offers. God wants us to have all of Him, just as He wants to have all of us. It is an honor to have Christ invest in us with His all.

I remember when a call from the police department sent me to a hospital in Topeka, Kansas. A man—we'll call him Dave—had gone into a bar with his ten-year-old son to confront another man who was there with Dave's wife. Unfortunately, it did not go as he had planned.

Dave made verbal fun of the other man, who then proceeded to beat him to a pulp. Before he knew it, Dave had been humiliated in front of his wife and son and had wound up in the ER. The police asked me to visit with Dave, but Dave was proud and was not interested in help or counsel. He wanted nothing to do with Christ. In fact, he did not want to talk to anyone. In spite of the fact that he hurt desperately, he opted to fight his battle alone.

How many people around us are doing the same thing? They ignore the person of Christ, who came to invest all He has in us, and instead end up fighting a lifetime of battles alone. My friend, if this is you, you are missing the power and honor of Almighty God.

The Glory of Indwelling

*I pray that out of his glorious riches he may strengthen you
with power through his Spirit in your inner being, so that
Christ may dwell in your hearts through faith. And I pray
that you, being rooted and established in love....*
—Ephesians 3:16–17

Why is there so much emphasis on strengthening? Certainly, it is for productivity, but there is also an inner strengthening so that Christ can dwell in our hearts by faith. When we invite Christ into our hearts, He is interested in creating a whole new person. He does not want patchwork Christians. He does not patch us; He creates a new heart in us. We may simply want to be patched, but He wants a much deeper, strengthened connection, so He gives us a new heart.

In Psalm 51:10–12, David prayed:

*Create in me a pure heart, O God, and renew a steadfast
spirit within me. Do not cast me from your presence or take
your Holy Spirit from me. Restore to me the joy of your salvation and grant me a willing spirit, to sustain me.*

Here is a cry not for a patch job, but for a completely new heart, a heart that would be strong and spiritually sustaining. Christ is interested in recreating something that will last.

The word for *dwell* in Ephesians 3:17 literally means "to take up residence; to settle down; to house permanently."[30] When Christ rebuilds our lives, He is not looking for a summer cottage. His investment is an eternal one. Do you see why we need to be strengthened with power? How can we, as mere mortals, support the presence of Almighty God living within us if we do not have supernatural help? We need His power to make that possible.

This lasting structure is not without personal responsibility on our part. Christ dwells in us through faith. I like to define faith as picking up the sacred pieces, the broken pieces, the crumbling pieces of your life and entrusting them to the Lord, believing that He will care for them. This bold faith implies a change in ownership. What was once yours becomes His.

I remember when Queenie and I bought our first home. It was exciting for us. In spite of a multitude of problems, we could look around and say, "This is ours." That home took on the look and feel of a refuge, a place of security. We could do whatever we wanted with it, so we cared for it and improved it. We put energy and effort into making it better and better.

Think about your house. You are much more in tune with what happens inside your four walls than in your neighbor's house or your place of employment. You remember to turn off the lights, you are conscious of damage, and you dream of ways to improve upon what you have been given.

When Christ takes up residence in our hearts, He wants the same kind of experience. He wants to take the lead because it's His temple, so we must give Him ownership. We must hand Him the keys.

This goes against our human nature. We want control. We think that we know what is best. However, when there is a holy ownership, you will find that you are more careful about your spiritual growth. When there is damage, you will seek to get it repaired right away. There will be no limit to the number of improvements that are possible. Holy ownership brings a positive sense of responsibility that will lift all areas of your life.

Becoming a Sanctuary for Christ

...in your inner being, so that Christ may dwell in your hearts through faith.
—Ephesians 3:16–17

God desires to house Himself, His holiness, in the context of relationship. A person's taste is reflected in his house. Similarly, God desires to be reflected in His temple, our souls. We need to be living examples of the image of God, and everything about us should reflect the One who made us. This intimacy is part of the immeasurably more. We are not meant to experience God from a distance. That's why Jesus came: to close the gap between humanity and God. Jesus changes us when we invite Him into our lives. *Jesus fills the hole of man with the whole of God.*

The word *heart* in this passage speaks to all of the thoughts and feelings we possess, our mental and moral activity. Paul used it figuratively to address all of those hidden areas of our lives. When you read this passage, think of *heart* as the seat of your desires and affections. These are things that, if you are really honest, you long for and hold dear. No wonder God wants this under His control! When the heart is in His control, we begin to experience the "more" in life.

Jesus fills the hole of man with the whole of God.

With the presence of Christ in your life and heart, you will have a direct connection to God's supernatural support system. You will have structure to help carry the weight of life. Trials come; they do. Problems pour out on top of us. Life can be hard, but when the Spirit is in control, He helps to shoulder those burdens and gives you the warmth of His comfort in trials.

As He shoulders your burdens, you will find that He replaces feelings of stress and unease with peace and comfort. It's a beautiful trade that only He can orchestrate. Imagine peace in the midst of a dark diagnosis. Imagine comfort after you have lost your job, declared bankruptcy, or lost your house. The Spirit calms us in ways that do not seem possible outside of the immeasurably more. We discover that there is more to life than we thought.

Not only will the Spirit comfort you, He will also allow you to see through to the other side. You will have the vision to see through the foggy and dark times of life. With Him in control, you will have hope. You will know that the darkness of today will not last forever. You will know that the problems you are facing are not the end of your story.

You will have the forgiveness from God necessary to cleanse your sins. Imagine being mentally free of your wrongdoings. Imagine going to sleep at night and not worrying about the things you did years ago or even the other day.

You will have the security and glory of His presence. When the Spirit is in control, you will find Him to be an active part of your life. He will be with you, no question about it. With His presence will come peace, direction, and communion with God.

Remember that the "glorious riches" in Ephesians 3:16–17 are Christ giving of Himself, His presence. Do you know what it's like to experience the glory of His indwelling? It is not wondering what to do with a small piece of God or a religion. It is not attempting to be spiritual from a distance or putting on an act for others. It is having the whole person of God filling your entire being. There is no social distancing with God, no fear of a spiritual virus. His presence is purifying and holy. In His presence, we find peace.

Standing at the Door

I remember well the dating process that Queenie and I experienced. One of the most frustrating aspects of it came at the end of a date. I had to go home, though I desperately wanted to be with her all the time. Eventually, we got engaged, but the frustrations continued. At the end of the evening, I had to leave. Finally, on June 2, 1973, we were married, and we took up residence together. The depth of our relationship changed greatly once that happened.

Are you engaged to Christ, or have you allowed Him to take up permanent residence in your life? Is He dwelling within you as an active part of your day, or is He standing outside the door, waiting for visiting hours to begin?

Christ wants to ignite your spiritual fires with power. He longs to invest in you through the Holy Spirit and take up permanent residence in your heart. It is the whole of God taking over the whole of man. Only then can you understand the power of a holy relationship with Christ. If you only want a piece of God, you will not understand what it's like to experience the peace of God.

Chapter Six Questions

Question: *Those who want only a piece of God cannot experience the peace of God.* Have you fallen into the "whole" of God? Are you just visiting Christ here and there at your convenience, or have you allowed Him to take up permanent residence in your life? What steps can you take to allow Christ to be an active part of your everyday life?

_____

_____

_____

_____

_____

_____

_____

_____

_____

Question: What is the current condition of your spiritual life? Are you spiritually fit or out of shape? Are you replenishing your spiritual tank so that you won't burn out? Are you exercising your spiritual muscles and applying the Word of God to your life? What changes do you need to make to enhance your spiritual fitness?

_____

_____

_____

_____

_____

_____

_____

_____

_____

_____

_____

Question: What do you think you desire more: what God has or who He is? Do you want Him to give you gifts without growing your relationship with Him? Do you want signs and wonders more than fellowship with the person of the Holy Spirit? Do you want earthly security more than spiritual security? Do you want comfort more than you want to learn how to be compassionate? What do your answers to these questions reveal about the true motives and desires of your heart?

_____

_____

_____

_____

_____

_____

_____

_____

_____

_____

_____

Action: *We need to be living examples of the image of God, and everything about us should reflect the One who made us.* You are the temple of the Holy Spirit, the dwelling place of the Most High God. God wants to be reflected in and through your life. Ask God to show you if you are a living example of His image and character. If need be, allow Him to do some "redecorating." Allow Him to show you the things in your life that need to be changed to reflect Him better. Then make those changes from a place of love and obedience.

Chapter Six Notes

_____

_____

_____

_____

_____

_____

_____

_____

_____

_____

_____

_____

_____

_____

_____

_____

_____

_____

_____

_____

_____

_____

_____

CHAPTER SEVEN

Knee-Deep in a Bottomless Pit

...so that Christ may dwell in your hearts through faith.
And I pray that you, being rooted and established in love,
may have power, together with all the Lord's holy people,
to grasp how wide and long and high and deep is the love
of Christ....

—***Ephesians 3:17–18***

Swimming and water are things I have always enjoyed. Just lying in cool water and relaxing on a hot day is, for me, next to heaven. When I am in a pool and I need to pass the time, it's always fun to walk from one end of the pool to the other. I start in the shallow end and keep walking. When I am in over my head, I tread water in such a way as to appear to be walking, even when the bottom of the pool is far below my feet. It gives the impression of strolling through the deep.

There are many Christians who like to give the impression that they have the ability to stroll effortlessly through the deep waters of the gospel, as if it's not a particularly challenging feat. Some are excited when they get up to their necks in truth. Others hold back and attempt to remain only knee-deep. The irony is that when it comes to the person, power, glory, and expanse of God, there is no such thing as knee-deep.

We cannot engage with God without being in over our heads! People who try to avoid the depths are in danger of drowning in the shallows.

We need a tide of spiritual revival and understanding to sweep over us and our churches, but seldom are we willing to invest what that requires. We live in an "instant age" in which we can have everything we want at the touch of a finger. We are so used to things happening instantly that we take that expectation into our faith. We look for quick solutions to spiritual lethargy, so revival is sometimes viewed as a microwave solution. "If we could just have a revival, everything would be better," or so we think. We forget that there is a cost to discipleship.

Yes, we need the instant transformation, but we also need the long-term commitment to obedience. We cannot live in the shallows of our limited understanding and expect to do great things for the Lord. We must dive into the deep before we drown in the shallows of our spiritual understanding. We cannot wade where the water is over our heads.

Dig In When It's Over Your Head

...being rooted and established in love....
—Ephesians 3:17

Whenever I am swimming in a deep lake, it's tempting to explore, but before I do so, I need to get my bearings. I want to know where the boat is anchored or how far from solid ground I may be.

We have already established that the realm of God is vast and infinite. Before there can be any profitable spiritual exploration, we must first be, as this passage says, "rooted and established." We need to be firmly planted and to have laid a foundation. There needs to be a continuance in the faith. In today's culture, people talk about being spiritual, but that does not mean they are Christ followers. They may be open to exploring a variety of religions, often as an intellectual or informational journey, but they are not rooted or grounded in God's truth. They are merely skirting about in a boat of curiosity. The reality is that it will not take much for that boat to sink or get mired on a sandbar of deception. That's what this passage is warning against.

Paul stressed the importance of being rooted and grounded in Christ. We are to be centered in Christ. How do we find the center of infinity? How do we become centered in a God who has no boundaries? We become centered in a relationship with Him. Christ gives us discernment and wisdom. He enables us to see beyond the nice-looking spiritual veneers Satan throws before us. This is how He grounds us.

"Being rooted and established" also gives us confidence in times of difficulty. It's not unusual to want to run when something seems overwhelming or frightening. When we do not understand all of the "whys" of life, it can create insecurity, so we look for escape hatches. Some even run from God because they fear His magnitude and mystery. Instead of running, we need to dig in.

Though the water may be over our heads, safety is not out of our reach. I may not be able to touch the top and bottom of the nature of God at the same time, but I can touch a portion of it at any time. The Lord wants to lead us into His presence through a discovery of all that He is. When we accept Christ, that journey begins and will continue throughout all of eternity.

It is mind-boggling to think that we will spend all of eternity being introduced to new dimensions of who God is and how He works. We must not make the faulty assumption that as soon as we get to heaven, we will become omniscient. If that were true, then we would become God, and that won't happen. There will always be room to learn.

> *We will spend all of eternity learning what God already knows and never catch up.*

Roots are like explorers. The roots of most trees bore deep into the soil, spreading out as they go. These rooting systems are strong and have depth and breadth to them. When we are rooted in Christ, we have a similar system of support. We grow and stretch and learn. Whether we are new Christians or veteran saints, our roots and branches will always be spreading out for the glory of God.

This is *why* we must be rooted, but please note that this verse gives specific direction as to *where* we need to be rooted: in *agape* love, which is the most perfect expression of love.

Six Truths About Love

It's common to think that the goal is to be rooted in knowledge, wisdom, spiritual gifts, a good church, Bible trivia, or famous speakers. However, God wants us to be "rooted and established" in *Him*, in love (Ephesians 3:17). After all, "God *is* love" (1 John 4:8, emphasis added). It is only from that base that we can address life. It's from that foundation that we can bring compassion and understanding into our relationships.

There are six key truths that we must keep in mind when it comes to *agape* love.

Love does not function independently of a relationship. It's not a stand-alone trait. You cannot have love and sit in isolation. That's not how it works! There must be more than one person involved. It demands to be shared, to be offered from one person to another.

Love draws others in. There is something magnetic about a person who lives in *agape* love. People are pulled in. They can't get enough. They want to be around that person as much as possible.

Love remembers, but it does not hold on to the negative. Love remembers the value of others, and it expresses that value to them. It remembers the sacrifice of love that Christ made for us, and it longs to live that out. Having this mindset of Christ means that love keeps no record of wrongs. It forgives and moves on. It remembers that every person is worthy of the love of Christ, no matter what.

Love comes with responsibility. It does not sit idly on a shelf, demanding attention. Love understands its role in breathing life into others, and it takes this responsibility very seriously. It serves; it gives. Love focuses on what it can offer rather than what it has to gain.

Because of that, **love renounces that which would tear relationships apart and belittle others**. It renounces what is abhorrent to God because God is love. Love pushes against envy, anger, resentment, and all other things that destroy and that go against the desires of Christ.

Sin will always creep in as long as we are fallen human beings, but **love comes through with restoration and**

righteousness. God forgives and rebuilds us, and we can offer that same forgiveness and hope to others through Christ. That is the nature of love.

For more than twenty years, Professor Edwin R. Keedy of the University of Pennsylvania Law School would start his first class by putting two figures on the blackboard.[31] He would write *4* and *2*. Then he would ask, "What's the solution?"

One student would call out, "Six!" Another one would say, "Two." Then several would shout out, "Eight!"

Professor Keedy would shake his head in the negative, then point out their collective error. "All of you failed to ask the key question: What is the problem? Gentlemen, unless you know what the problem is, you cannot possibly find the answer."

Too often, we seek answers without really defining the problem. We feel that the answer is a lack of love, but we have not yet discovered that the problem is sin. When sin reigns in our lives, we cannot begin to understand the expanse of love. It's like going out into deep waters without any clue as to where we are or how to swim.

There is a critical need for the saints to be rooted in love, but there is more!

Grab Hold to Get It into Your Head

...may have power ... to grasp....
—Ephesians 3:18

When faced with the infinite scope of the person of God, it would be easy to think that knowing God at a deeper level would come with restricted access, that only the hyper-spiritual would be allowed the full experience or only a certain kind of saint would be permitted admittance. This Scripture lets us know that the opposite is true:

the understanding of God is not limited to a select few. We can "have power, *together with all the Lord's holy people*, to grasp…" (Ephesians 3:18, emphasis added).

Now, just because we know something does not mean that it has registered as a permanent truth in our minds. Many times, I have wished that I knew all I had been taught. I think of the years spent in school, years spent in study, yet so much information has leaked out of my brain like water through a sieve.

In this passage, Paul addressed the human tendency to let information slip away. He prayed that when it came to understanding the awesome nature of God, we would have the "power to grasp." Some translations read, "…may be able to comprehend" (Ephesians 3:18 NKJV, NASB). That is a more literal look at the text, but it still does not fully convey the power of this passage.

The word Paul used for *power* comes from a compound word used only once in the entire New Testament. Just to give you an idea of the power of the root word, I refer to Matthew 16:18: "…and on this rock I will build my church, and the gates of hell shall not prevail against it" (ESV).

The term for "not prevail"[32] employs the same root word used for *power* in Ephesians 3:18,[33] which is the Greek word *ischyō*.[34] In the Ephesians scripture, *power* comes in the form of a compound word that strengthens its punch. The meaning behind the compound word in Ephesians is "to have full strength, be entirely competent."[35] Full strength to do what? To comprehend, meaning to "grasp or take hold of; to possess as one's own."[36]

The Lord does not want the nature of His character to be an impersonal piece of knowledge that we hear about, nor does He want it to be reserved for a select few we label as theologians. He wants us to own the truth and make it personal to our own lives. Look again at Ephesians 3:17–

18: "...so that Christ may dwell in your hearts through faith. And I pray that you, being rooted and established in love, may have power, together with all the Lord's holy people, to grasp how wide and long and high and deep is the love of Christ...."

Paul wants us fully to grasp the understanding of the love of God "together with all the saints" (Ephesians 3:18 BSB). This understanding is not meant to be some private experience or a rare privilege, like a vision. Rather, it is a collective gift for everyone to savor.

In many areas of faith, we are able to walk successfully with Christ because of being in community with other believers. Even so, the love of God is meant to be not only shared by all of us, but also possessed completely by all of us. Do not hesitate to grab hold of all of God. He desires to have all of you, and there are consequences when we fail to enter into that full relationship.

English storyteller T. H. White recalls a boyhood experience in *The Book of Merlyn*: "My father made me a wooden castle big enough to get into, and he fixed real pistol barrels beneath its battlements to fire a salute on my birthday, but made me sit in front the first night ... to receive the salute. I, believing I was to be shot, cried."[37]

How many times, because of our lack of knowledge of the truth, have we misinterpreted the actions or the Word of God? Our lack of knowledge left us with the inability to discern what God intended. As a result, we acted out of shallow emotion rather than knowledgeable love. We thought that we were under attack when, in fact, God was inviting us into His presence for all of eternity.

Getting to know the Lord and His love will deepen you and your love. Are you ready to grab hold? Do so and get God's love into your head and heart, digging in when it's over your head.

Taking Off to Move Ahead

...may have power, together with all the Lord's holy people, to grasp how wide and long and high and deep is the love of Christ....

—Ephesians 3:18

The Apostle Paul painted a picture for us of the love of God. He wanted us to grasp the width, length, height, and depth of God's love. I don't think that Paul was attempting to be mysterious in this passage, nor was he attempting to nod to some other aspect of the faith. Very simply, he was pointing out that God's love is multidimensional.

It is good for us to examine the dimensions of our love for the Lord and His creation. Some simple questions can start this process. First, think about the breadth of your love. Are there people you exclude because they have hurt you or because they are too different? Perhaps they are not the right color, or they fall into a different socioeconomic class. Maybe they are not living the way you think they should. Maybe they are in a different age group. Perhaps you are so self-centered that you think others must enter your world before you can love them. Is God Himself excluded from your love and its expressions when the situations of life are not meeting your expectations or desires? In other words, do you stop loving God when life is not going as you think it should?

Now, what about the length of your love? Is it long-suffering and willing to put up with hurt after hurt? Will it go the extra mile for others? Does the love you demonstrate go beyond what you can do on your own as a human being?

What about the depth of your love? Is it easily shaken or blown away by pain or anger, or is it rooted deeply enough to withstand the assault of the enemy? Are your love roots based solely on what God does for you, or do they extend to the primary basis of love: who God is? Is your love a stabilizing factor for your family and friends and others who know you? What is the dependability factor of your love?

What about the height of your love? Does it elevate the quality of your life and the lives of those around you? Does it enable you to keep moving forward in your spiritual walk and not be overcome by a critical spirit? Does it cause Christ to be glorified, to be seen in a positive light in your life? Is it always reaching for higher heights in understanding and walking with God?

There must be a launching point in your walk with Christ, something that propels you forward to penetrate into the furthest expanse of the love of God. His love is vast! There is no need to stay in the shallows. The deeper you go, the more love you will know. There is more to life!

Off the Deep End

Some Christians are like children in a swimming pool. The very small children stick to the baby pool. When you get a little older, you advance to the big pool. When you begin to learn to swim, you head for deeper waters. When you feel confident enough, you take leaps off the diving board! You may be scared, but it's exciting to explore the depths in that way.

Often as Christians, when we step out of the baby pool, we don't get into the big pool. We walk down the street, and when we see a puddle, we splash ourselves and say, "Praise the Lord! I'm wet." When we do this, we miss the expanse of the love of God, and we are left with a version of Christianity that is shallow and without knowledge of who God really is.

Don't sit in a pool of water on the beach and fail to

jump into the ocean. Don't be afraid to move ahead. Don't be fearful of moving away from your sense of security. Begin to live in God's security!

It's time to jump into the deep end, where the water is over your head. It's time to grab hold of the love of God in all its fullness and take off into His expanse. If you don't, you are destined for pain. People who merely dabble in the depths are in danger of drowning in the shallows, and I am telling you: there is more to life!

WORKBOOK

Chapter Seven Questions

Question: What do you think is the most important thing in which to be rooted as a follower of Christ? Is your walk with Christ grounded in love? What would be the evidence of this?

_____

_____

_____

_____

_____

_____

_____

_____

_____

_____

_____

Question: Look at the six key truths about *agape* love: love does not function independently of a relationship, love draws others in, love remembers, love comes with responsibility, love renounces that which would tear relationships apart and belittle others, and love comes through with restoration and righteousness. Are these key truths characteristic of your relationships with others? In what ways does sin hinder you from entering into the full expanse of God?

_____

_____

_____

_____

_____

_____

_____

_____

_____

_____

Question: *Getting to know the Lord and His love will deepen you and your love.* Do you know that God loves you? What has He done in your life that has undeniably shown you His love? Is the love you have for God and others rooted in your relationship with God and an intimate knowledge of Him and His love for you?

_____

_____

_____

_____

_____

_____

_____

_____

_____

_____

_____

Action: Examine the dimensions of our love for the Lord and His creation. In a journal or notebook, answer the following questions about each dimension of your love for God and others.

- *The breadth of your love*: Are there people you exclude because they have hurt you or because they are too different? Do you stop loving God when life is not going according to your plan?

- *The length of your love*: Is your love long-suffering and willing to put up with hurt after hurt? Will it go the extra mile for others? Does the love you demonstrate go beyond what you can do on your own as a human being?

- *The depth of your love*: Is your love easily shaken or blown away by pain or anger? Are your love roots based solely on what God does for you, or do they extend to the primary basis of love: who God is? What is the dependability factor of your love?

- *The height of your love*: Does your love elevate the quality of your life and the lives of those around you? Does it cause Christ to be glorified, to be seen in a positive light in your life? Is it always reaching for higher heights in understanding and walking with God?

Chapter Seven Notes

_____

_____

_____

_____

_____

_____

_____

_____

_____

_____

_____

_____

_____

_____

_____

_____

_____

_____

_____

_____

_____

CHAPTER EIGHT

How Do You Fit a Boeing 747 into Your Garage?

Do you have a garage that is too big? No? I have never heard anyone say that a garage is too big. I mean, garages exist for us to put as much as we can into them. Often we have so much in our garages that there is no room for our cars. We have workbenches, tools, golf clubs, bikes, boxes, trash, freezers, refrigerators, you name it—it's all in the garage.

Some garages are built with higher entries so that boats or large trucks can be parked inside. Now, imagine trying to fit a Boeing 747 into your garage. The wingspan and total length of a 747 are over 200 feet each, and its height exceeds 60 feet. A 747 will seat hundreds of passengers. Do you think you could park that in your garage alongside your seven-seat minivan? A typical two-car garage is about 20 feet by 20 feet. That's not much room for the jet!

Okay, let's face it—if anyone were to talk seriously about parking a 747 in the garage, you would think that he was a moron. You would completely discount his words and think twice about any other ideas he might have. Our home garages were not built to hold Boeing 747s.

Here comes the rub. How can we be so brazen as to say that the infinite, unbound God can park and take up residence in our souls? It seems like we are too small to contain Him, but here is the good news: *you are a perfect fit for the presence of God.* We were made to be filled with the presence of God. We were created to be temples of the Almighty God, and as His Word says, "God is love" (1 John 4:8).

Love is one of the most sought-after longings of the heart. We desire to be wanted, to be accepted, to be loved. We have been taught that love is more than a feeling; it is also a decision. It is a commitment that never ends.

There are many who struggle with the concept of love in their own lives. If you grew up without experiencing unconditional love from those around you, then you struggle to understand godly love in your adult life. If there was abuse in the home, if you grew up in a place where the words "I love you" were seldom or never spoken, or if love was not demonstrated in a healthy fashion, then you carry that baggage into your adult life.

For others, love was frighteningly tied to sexual abuse, or it became an exchange of favors that left you feeling used. Friends stuck around as long as you laughed at the right times and cared about what they cared about and did whatever they wanted you to do, regardless of the cost.

You might have had a relationship in which the one holding you emotionally captive would say, "If you really love me, you'll do this." You might have craved love so desperately that you were willing to do anything, even though it left you feeling guilty, empty, and used. Your desire for acceptance blinded you to the fact that you had become a tool for someone else's gratification, and you are ashamed and saddened by that period of your life.

Not everyone has memories of love gone wrong, but every day, we all face decisions that have the potential to create either healthy or painful memories. Regardless of where we find ourselves in the spectrum of this quest for love, there is always room to grow.

The desire for love and acceptance is normal and healthy. Real, unconditional love does exist, not only with God, but also with many of His children. That love can be yours personally and permanently. The painful memories you have acquired in your search for love can be overcome by an intimate knowledge of the breadth of God's love for you.

Here is more good news: it is possible to know the love of God because our ability to know God is not limited to our personal experience or our intellectual capacity to understand. God, who is love, can park in your soul. He is a perfect fit for you and your life.

Read Ephesians 3:14–21 again:

> *For this reason I kneel before the Father, from whom every family in heaven and on earth derives its name. I pray that out of his glorious riches he may strengthen you with power through his Spirit in your inner being, so that Christ may dwell in your hearts through faith. And I pray that you, being rooted and established in love, may have power, together with all the Lord's holy people, to grasp how wide and long and high and deep is the love of Christ, and to know this love that surpasses knowledge—that you may be filled to the measure of all the fullness of God.*
>
> *Now to him who is able to do immeasurably more than all we ask or imagine, according to his power that is at work within us, to him be glory in the church and in Christ Jesus throughout all generations, for ever and ever! Amen.*

Knowing the Love of God

Know: to know and understand. To know through experience, thus having a practical knowledge.[38]

We have addressed how the Greek word for *know* means that there is a relationship between the person knowing and the person or object being known. It indicates value and an intimate familiarity.

If you were to look at me, you would see that my nose is always on the verge of a right turn. That's because I have broken my nose on four different occasions. I vividly remember spraining my ankle and having Queenie take me to the hospital ER for treatment. When the doctor came in, he looked at me and said, "It looks bad. Your nose is seriously broken."

"But Doc, it's my ankle!" I had to tell him.

Sometimes what appears to be obvious is the wrong answer. What most of us need is a spiritual "knows" job. We need to get our information straight about the person and the love of God. Only then can we fully enter into and accept His perfect love.

Intimacy

Intimacy involves entrusting and giving our deepest emotions and feelings and our goals and dreams to another person. It is holding the character of the one you love high and trusting his or her commitment to you. Intimacy is security in the most rugged and difficult of times in a marriage or a friendship. It is a sign of maturity.

Relationships mature as we spend more and more time and energy there. The more time I spend with Queenie, the deeper my knowledge of her becomes and the greater the level of intimacy we experience. The same goes for our relationship with God.

Paul prayed that we would know the love of God, that we would be intimately familiar with His love from experience. I don't want to be acquainted with the love of God only through someone's testimony. I want to be held by Him, forgiven by Him, desired by Him. That's the kind of intimacy Paul was getting at.

This word *know* also indicates that what is known is of value to the one who knows it. The love of God is a valuable truth to me. It is firsthand knowledge that I treasure. I value His love for me and His presence in my life, and because of that, I seek to go deeper in my knowledge of and intimacy with God.

For me to tell you that Queenie loves me is a fact you would assume as a given. We have been together for a very long time, and I speak very highly of her. Nevertheless, the fact that Queenie loves me is very valuable knowledge to me. Not only do I *know* that she loves me, I also savor it and experience it firsthand. This experiential love is part of what Paul was talking about, but he did not stop there.

Paul prayed that we would know the love of God that surpasses knowledge. This again emphasizes a personal encounter. It surpasses or exceeds expectations. It goes beyond. What does it go beyond? Knowledge.

*Paul prayed that we would know
that which is beyond knowing,
that which is beyond knowledge.*

What a fascinating way to pray!

Knowledge

In this context, knowledge is not obtained by intellectual activity, but rather by the operation of the Holy Spirit. So, how can we possibly know the love of God without being involved with Him? How can we expect to plunge the depths of His love without His Spirit at work in us?

We crave intimacy. We long for personal attention. There isn't a day that passes that we do not look for some sort of intimate response from the one we love. So, why are we negligent in seeking intimacy with Christ?

Prior to our wedding, Queenie and I wrote countless letters to each other, spilling our hearts and emotions all over the paper. I was studying in Israel, and she was in the U. S. We expressed our love with poetic eloquence, but frankly, it wasn't enough. I wanted to know Queenie not by letter, but by living with her. I wanted to breathe her sorrows and inhale her joys and listen to her heartbeat—in person. I wanted to know her in a way that went beyond textbook romance.

In the same way, I do not want my relationship with Christ to be determined by a theologian I never met or a Bible scholar who does not know me from the mail carrier. If I expect to be filled with the love of God, I need to know *Him*. I appreciate the message from the pastor and the lesson from the teacher, but I do not want their knowledge of God to be the basis of my love for God. Their insight can open doors of understanding, but their words cannot do what being personally engaged with Christ will do. I want to know Him personally.

There's a story of a businessman at a meeting in an up-scale restaurant. While there, he met Lee Iacocca.[39]

"Mr. Iacocca," he gushed, "the American business hero! I've studied your career, and any success I've had comes from emulating you. Would you do me a favor? I'm with some colleagues. Please come by my table, say 'Hello, Harry,' and let me introduce you. It would mean so much to me."

Iacocca agreed. He waited for the man to sit down and then walked towards his table.

"Holy smoke!" cried one of Harry's friends. "It's Lee

Iacocca, and he's heading this way!"

"Hello, Harry!" Iacocca said. "Introduce me to your friends."

Harry looked at him blankly. "Come back later, Lee," he said. "Can't you see we're trying to have some lunch!"

Do you really want to know the Lord, or do you want to use Him to make you look good? Don't ever attempt to pass God off as a casual acquaintance. Rather, seek to know Him in the way Paul urged in Ephesians 3.

Knowing the Love of God Requires an Overflowing Tank

...filled to the measure of all the fullness of God.
—Ephesians 3:19

We are to know the love of God so we will be filled. The Greek word used for *filled* means to be full, satisfied, whole, or useful.[40]

> *Not only can we know what is beyond knowing, but we can also be filled with what cannot be contained.*

Years ago, when the price of gas did not require a second mortgage, it was not unusual to pull into a gas station and order a dollar's worth of gas. We felt no need to fill the tank; a dollar's worth would do. The problem with many Christians is that they are satisfied with only an hour's worth of God on Sunday or a crisis's worth of grace and strength. Conversely, the Lord is never satisfied with saints who attempt to go the distance without the necessary resources or with minimal strength. He wants us to be *full*.

The word used for *fullness* in this passage is interesting. The way it is used refers to that which fills up or that which has been completed.[41] This word speaks not only of being filled, but of being whole.

> *In being filled with the love of God,*
> *we find not only satisfaction, but also*
> *a sense of being whole and useful.*

Let me remind you that this is not a prayer to be filled with the gifts of the Spirit, special abilities, or anything else God gives. It all centers on who God is and who we can be in Him. Paul was praying that we would be filled with God Himself.

Have you noticed how much filling we deal with in our everyday lives? The cream in a donut, cotton in an aspirin bottle, air in a big bag of chips that holds very few chips, promises made by politicians who will never come close to fulfilling them. People also throw filler into their spiritual lives, only to discover that it does not leave a lasting taste or benefit. We attempt to fill our spirits with emotional highs, physical manifestations of God's power, or holy talk that's nothing more than just talk. We are also filled with things that cause problems, such as anger, resentment, revenge, unforgiveness, arrogance, and selfishness.

Consider the story of a sinking ship. The people onboard are scrambling to save themselves. One man named Joe says, "Woman the lifeboats! Woman the lifeboats!" Moe responds, "You don't 'woman' the lifeboats. You 'man' the lifeboats." Joe fires back, "You fill your lifeboats, and I'll fill mine."[42]

Let's not kid ourselves. Some of us are doing exactly what this story indicates. We are trying to fill our lives with only what we want, with things that give us a temporary thrill. As a result, we find ourselves empty right after we finish putting in our filling.

With what do you desire to fill your life? Do you want to fill yourself up with an unsatisfying version of Christianity, or do you want to fill up on that which will give eternal satisfaction and life, that which is found only in Christ?

I want you to think about the effects of the fullness of God. Who can actually contain all the fullness of God? None of us. That's why in being filled with the fullness of God, we become overflowing reservoirs of grace. People who are filled with the fullness of God cannot help but spill over into the lives of others in a refreshing way. Are you an overflowing tank, filled with the fullness of God and spilling over into the lives of others?

Listen again to the admonition and prayer of Paul. He asked that we would come "to know this love that surpasses knowledge" so we "may be filled to the measure of all the fullness of God" (Ephesians 3:19).

Do you want to be full? If you commit yourself to knowing God, you will experience a genuine love that fills you up and overflows to others. There is more to life!

WORKBOOK

Chapter Eight Questions

Question: In your life, have the people around you loved you well? Have they loved you unconditionally? Is the concept of love comforting or difficult for you? What traumas in your past might have kept you hesitant to open yourself to receive God's love?

_____

_____

_____

_____

_____

_____

_____

_____

_____

_____

Question: *Relationships mature as we spend more and more time and energy there.* Do you feel secure in your relationship with God and His love for you, even when you experience the most rugged and difficult times in life? How does your level of security in God reveal the level of maturity in your relationship with Him? The amount of time and energy spent on your relationship with God can be indicative of the maturity and intimacy of the relationship. What does the amount of time and energy you spend on God convey about your relationship with Him?

Question: Are you negligent in seeking intimacy with Christ? Do you think that it is possible to know and experience the love of God without being involved with Him? Have you invited the Holy Spirit to work in you and plunge you into the depths of God's love? If so, what did

He reveal to you through that? If not, what is holding you back?

_____

_____

_____

_____

_____

_____

_____

_____

_____

_____

_____

Action: *I want you to think about the effects of the fullness of God. Who can actually contain all the fullness of God?* You cannot contain the fullness of God's love, which means that it is going to spill out of you into other people's lives. Ask God to fill you with His love to overflowing, then ask Him to show you a specific way you can share that love with someone in your life.

Chapter Eight Notes

CHAPTER NINE

A System of "Waits" and Measures

Being patient in our spiritual walk enables us to see miracles in our spiritual work. Right now, there are tons of people on a diet. We desire to have a waistline instead of a shoreline, to be able to enter into a conversation without weighing more than our words, to see our shoes without the help of a periscope, and to wear clothes without leaving marks. You know what I'm talking about.

Dieting isn't easy. I mean, what do you do when there is a big, scrumptious coconut cream pie topped with just the right texture and consistency of whipped cream staring you in the face? Give it away? No! You eat it and are grateful that you dieted for the past two hours, thus making room for that pie. Then what happens? The next day, you whine because the scales don't record any victories.

The biggest problem with diets is that our weight does not come off as fast as we think it should. We establish our goals, then fight valiantly to reach our second-week goal by the end of the tenth week. We continue to be more "roly" than "poly." Impatience has wrecked many a diet.

Our impatience in life is not limited to diet and waist-line results. We are impatient Christians, too. We have lost too much "wait." We want results, and we want them now. One of the greatest gains for the church would be to put on some "wait."

In our Christian walk, life is a system of "waits" and measures. Unless we are willing to wait on the Lord, listen to Him, serve Him, and follow Him, we will find ourselves unable to measure the work of the Holy Spirit and the effectiveness of our own walk with Jesus Christ correctly and productively. So, let's look into some important truths about waiting on the Lord.

His Ability Exceeds Our Inability

> *Now to him who is able to do immeasurably more than all we ask or imagine, according to his power that is at work within us....*
> **—Ephesians 3:20**

It is important for us to be reminded of the context of this text. Paul was praying that we would be able to grasp and comprehend the full scope of the love of God so that we could be filled with His fullness.

Most of us read that and think, *"Okay, no problem"*—that is, until we think of that one person we can't stomach. Suddenly the need to grasp the love of God becomes real. Then another reality hits. I have run into countless Christians who determine that they cannot understand God or love like He loves.

Look again at the closing words of this great prayer:

> *Now to Him who is able to do exceedingly abundantly above all that we ask or think....*
> **—Ephesians 3:20** *(NKJV)*

When it comes to the practical application of this prayer, Paul calmed our fears by pointing out that God is greater than our weaknesses. We spend so much time complaining about our inhibitions and weaknesses that we forget about the power of God. His ability exceeds our inability. As far as our ineptness would stretch on a measuring rod of inability, God's power stretches further on a scale of ability.

A literal rendering of the beginning of this verse would read, "…to Him who is able, above all things…." In fact, the word used for *able* means "power."[43] Paul was saying that God has the power to make things happen. He has more power than positive thinking, more power than human ability, more power than meditation, more power than religion, more power than anything or anyone else.

One of the mistakes we make is to base our theology, our view of God, on human weaknesses.

Our view of God tends to reflect our frailties more than God's strength. We need to see what God can do, not what we cannot do.

Paul made it clear that God has the ability not only to get the job done, but to get it done in a way that exceeds what is expected. God will do exceedingly more, abundantly more, immeasurably more. God can give you and me the ability to love and make it so you and I can love in a way greater than we ever dreamed possible.

How? Through coming to grips with an understanding of God. Ephesians 3:20 is not saying that God can "do exceedingly abundantly above all that we ask or think" (NKJV) as it relates to filling our earthly treasure chests.

He is able to do more than we can imagine as it relates to the joys of knowing Him and living with Him.

Some of us are so bogged down in the follies of earthly relationships that we cannot imagine anything greater than what is. We cannot fathom how there could be something better than what is before us, but God can "do immeasurably more" (Ephesians 3:20). There is no human yardstick capable of defining:

- The extent to which we are able to forgive and be forgiven

- The extent to which we can give and encourage

- The changes and transformations that can occur in us regardless of our past

- The patience we exhibit where we once fumed with intolerance

- The quantity of tithes and offerings we can give to the Lord, beyond what we think we can afford

God's ability exceeds our inability.

Max Lucado is a superb writer. He possesses the ability to paint our emotions on paper and to take a piece of spiritual bread that has been crusted over with the winds of apathy and make it fresh. In one chapter of his book *No Wonder They Call Him the Savior*, he deals with guilt, the all too familiar, menacing consequence of sin. Lucado talks about the sin of Adam and Eve and how they attempted to cope with their guilt by hiding and passing the buck. All of mankind was cursed from that point on. The hearts of so many grew cold because that was the only way they knew how to deal with guilt. Lucado wrote:[44]

> If only we had a guilt-kidney that could pass on our failures or a built-in eraser that would help us live with ourselves. But we don't. In fact, that is precisely the problem. Man cannot cope with guilt alone. When man was created, he was created without the ability to cope with guilt. Why? Because he was not made to make mistakes. But when he did, he had no way to deal with it. The cross did what sacrificed lambs could not do. It erased our sins not for a year, but for eternity ... [and] you can't do that by yourself. I don't care how many worship services you attend or good deeds you do, your goodness is insufficient. You can't be good enough to deserve forgiveness. No one bats a thousand. No one bowls 300. No one ... [and] that's why we have guilt in the world. That's why we need a Savior... [because] two kids in a mud puddle can't clean each other. They need someone spotless.

His Work Expands in Our Wait

Look at the results of your work for the Lord. If you could remove God from the process of what you have done, would the results be any different? Much of what we do for the Lord is exactly that; it is what *we* have done, not what God has done through us. We have tapped our gifts to the max, but we are not tapping into the Giver. Think about it.

What are you currently doing that makes any demands on the power of God?

The truth that God does more than we ask or imagine is further clarified as to *how* He does this: "…according to his power that is at work within us" (Ephesians 3:20). This is not a particularly easy pill to swallow. Usually, we are not looking to see results from a power within, but rather from a power without.

We want to see what would happen in our marriage if our spouse were to change his or her ways or become more understanding or listen better, if the kids would not interfere, if the schedules were different, or if the financial strain were less. We want to see what would happen to our career if we were to have a better boss, live in a bigger city, have better opportunities for advancement, or get a better education. We want to see what would happen in our church if we were to have a more dynamic pastor and better and more tithers or if our church were to function the way we think it should.

Most of our focus is on the external. It's on other people and things, not on ourselves. We need to understand that God can do the impossible and unimaginable "according to his power that is at work *within* us" (Ephesians 3:20, emphasis added). This is where the wait comes in. Most of us are not willing to wait upon the Lord in order to make this happen.

It's hard to strike a balance between human leadership and godly power. Seminars teach that good leaders make things happen. That is true to a point. However, if I were only interested in what I could accomplish, I would enter another line of work.

The power at work within me must be the power of God. As a result, I must also remember that God has a timetable that is not always the same as mine. When we rush ahead without really spending time with the Lord in prayer, we are not operating in a productive, Christ-honoring fashion. All too often, we are so impatient that we design, manufacture, and implement a plan while talking *about* Christ without involving Him in it.

When it comes to spiritual influence, if you want to carry weight, you need to learn to wait. This is not waiting in the sense of killing time. We need to enter the conscious presence of God in prayer and in the Bible, allowing Him to speak to us and give us direction. He speaks through His Word and through His Spirit to our thoughts. We wait in His presence for His answers.

Sometimes I have to ask myself, "Is my time with the Lord comprised of throwing a few words at the door of the prayer closet and thinking that I've done my duty? Is it speed-reading through a few verses in the Bible and closing it with a sense of 'Well, that's done'? Have I allowed my intimate time with the Savior to be little more than a hassle or interruption in my day?"

At times, yes, I have been guilty of all of this. When that happens, my only response is to pray, "Forgive me, Lord, and help me not to allow the enemy, Satan, to pull me from Your presence. I don't simply want to hang around Christ. I want to be in Him and to let Him live in me. I must wait in His presence for His answers and His direction."

A great deal is done through intercessory prayer. Some people think that prayer is like a magic trick. Simply pray, and voila! Their dreams come true. The answers to their shopping list come to life. Others think that prayer is a waste of time and there is no need to bother. Then there are those who treat it like a religious ritual, something you do because you are a Christian.

In reality, prayer is many things, not the least of which is the doorway into the expanse of God. God handed us His private number and said, "Call any time." When we call, He listens. When I enter into serious prayer, it's like I have gone through the door and am lost in His infinite love. I am overwhelmed. I am overjoyed. In Christ, I have overcome.

This experience, and so much more, is possible for all believers. The key is that we have to be careful not to stop praying before God is done working. We stop praying because we feel it's time, but it is a mistake to assume that our instincts are indicators of God's will.

Can you trust your instincts? Many think that they can. They think that going with their gut or making decisions based on a hunch is often the best way to proceed. Based on the discernment level of most people, maybe they should rethink that approach. Instinct is influenced heavily by the things that nourish it.

What nourishes your instincts? Is it your appetites? Is it your relationship with Christ? Is it your emotions? Is it your ability to reason? Is it your ability to see the big picture? Can you look objectively at life without being swayed by anger, bitterness, or past hurts?

The bottom line is that you need to admit who or what controls you because whoever or whatever controls you controls your instincts. I read years ago that desires born in a close relationship with Christ can be trusted. Our instincts need to learn to follow Christ before we start following them.

There is an internal power that must be at work within us before we become an external force for the Lord. What kind of power is at work within you? Is it personal drive? Peer pressure? Monetary or material greed? Rebellion? Lust? A spirit of revenge? Unresolved conflicts? A need for independence? Laziness? There is so much that the Lord wants to do in us and through us, but we must wait upon Him and align with Him in order to move with Him.

God's work is expanded in our wait. He so empowers us that we become unmistakable products of His presence. He breathes new life into us and becomes a power that breaks forth in our lives. All of this comes from waiting.

His Glory Expands in Our Obedience

*...to him be glory in the church and in Christ Jesus through-
out all generations, for ever and ever! Amen.*
—Ephesians 3:21

This line of Paul's prayer is significant. He cited God's glory in the church and in Christ. What is this glory? It is the manifestation of the character of God. When we are comprehending and grasping the love and person of God, when we are becoming a spiritual force to reckon with because of the power at work within us, when we are surrendered to the Lord wholly and completely, then the glory of God is seen by those around us.

Look at the picture Paul drew for us. The glory of God exhales in our obedience. Too often, we simply exchange the guilt of disobedience for the glory of obedience, but it needs to be more than that. Glory must be rooted in Christ, ongoing and overflowing. The desire of Paul's prayer is that the glory of God would be evident throughout all generations forever. It's a desire not simply to escape what is wrong, but to immerse ourselves in what is right and holy. That is long-term obedience.

How much godly glory is visible in your life? How much are you allowing the character of God to be demonstrated in and through you? There is glory in the church when there is glory in the believer because believers are the essence of the church.

In prayer, we take the time to inhale the presence, power, and person of God. The Lord would also like to exhale His glory through us. Are you ready? Are you obedient?

Consider the story of G. Campbell Morgan:[45]

[G.] Campbell Morgan was one of 150 young men who sought entrance to the Wesleyan ministry in 1888. He passed the doctrinal examinations, but then faced the trial sermon. In a cavernous auditorium that could seat more than 1,000 sat three ministers and 75 others who came to listen.

When Morgan stepped into the pulpit, the vast room and the searching, critical eyes caught him up short. Two weeks later Morgan's name appeared among the 105 RE-JECTED for the ministry that year.

Jill Morgan, his daughter-in-law, wrote in her book, *A Man of the Word*, "He wired to his father the one word, 'Rejected,' and sat down to write in his diary: 'Very dark everything seems. Still, He knoweth best.' Quickly came the reply: 'Rejected on earth. Accepted in heaven. Dad.'"

...Rejection is rarely permanent, as Morgan went on to prove. Even in this life, circumstances change, and ultimately, there is no rejection of those accepted by Christ.

If we wait, God will use us. G. Campbell Morgan went on to become a great preacher whose influence remains to this day.

Are you having trouble in your spiritual walk because you have lost too much "wait"? If so, you have lost the ability to measure your spiritual effectiveness. Patience enables us to see miracles in our spiritual walk. Don't allow hasty actions to lead you away from God's will or past failures to bog you down. There is more to life!

WORKBOOK

Chapter Nine Questions

Question: *We spend so much time complaining about our inhibitions and weaknesses that we forget about the power of God. His ability exceeds our inability.* Are you more focused on your shortcomings and inabilities than on God's power? How has your insecurity and self-doubt affected your relationship with God and your ability to serve Him fully?

_____

_____

_____

_____

_____

_____

_____

_____

_____

_____

Question: Are you content with the status quo? Have you settled into the comfort zone of your life to the point where you are not interested in or looking for the "more" God has for you? Are you bogged down and distracted by the cares of this world, allowing them to take your focus off of God's vision? Think about the current trajectory of your life and ask God to show you a glimpse of the "immeasurably more" He wants for you. What does He reveal?

_____

_____

_____

_____

_____

_____

_____

_____

_____

_____

Question: Can you walk out your current lifestyle in your own strength? What are you doing that makes a demand on the power of God? In what ways does God want to change and empower you rather than change your circumstances or those around you? Are you willing to wait on Him to make that happen?

_____

_____

_____

_____

_____

_____

_____

_____

_____

_____

_____

_____

Action: *In reality, prayer is many things, not the least of which is the doorway into the expanse of God.* Are you willing to wait in the presence of God? Are you willing to allow Him to make His glory visible in your life? How much are you allowing the character of God to be demonstrated in and through you?

Devote yourself to a time of prayer and ask God to reveal to you the answers to the following questions:

- Does my time with the Lord consist of throwing a few words at the door of the prayer closet and thinking that I have done my duty?

- Do I merely speed-read through a few verses in the Bible and close it with a sense of "Well, that's done"?

- Have I allowed my intimate time with the Savior to be little more than a hassle or interruption in my day?

As God shows you your heart in these areas, if you find yourself lacking in any of them, pray something like this: "Forgive me, Lord, and help me not to allow the enemy, Satan, to pull me from Your presence. I don't simply want to hang around Christ. I want to be in Him and to let Him live in me. I must wait in His presence for His answers and His direction."

Chapter Nine Notes

_____

_____

_____

_____

_____

_____

_____

_____

_____

_____

_____

_____

_____

_____

_____

_____

_____

_____

_____

_____

_____

_____

CONCLUSION

It's Your Time

There's an old story about a guy who was wandering through a country cemetery at night and fell into an empty grave that had been dug the day before in preparation for a funeral. After about thirty minutes of trying to jump, claw, and climb his way out, he gave up, exhausted, and sat back in a corner of the grave to wait until morning.

A few minutes later, a farmer hunting raccoons came along and fell into the same hole. He didn't realize that there was someone else in the hole with him, so he attempted to climb out of the hole on his own. After he had jumped and clawed for a few minutes with no success, the first man reached out from the dark corner, placed a hand on the farmer's shoulder, and said, "You'll never make it." But he did!

The first man who fell in had a defeated attitude. Because of his own inability, he was not able to see what was possible with both of them in the hole. He didn't realize that the power to overcome was available to them both. The farmer *did* make it out of the hole before morning.[46]

You would be surprised at God's ability to enable us to live obediently. We can do it by His power. We decide, and He enables.

We must build upon our foundation, first establishing our faith. To faith, we add goodness, then knowledge, then self-control, then perseverance, then godliness, then mutual affection, then love. Once we have these building blocks of character, we must continue growing. It's not enough to possess some love or godliness. We must continue to evolve and seek holiness in each of these areas.

To do this, we must submit to God every day, giving everything over to Him and making Him our only focus. We must seek the whole of God, never settling for a piece of Him or a mere glimpse of all He is and has to offer. We must dive into His depths, knowing that He wants us to explore His vastness and that He will reveal Himself to and guide any saint who dares to go deep. We must believe that He can take us beyond our human limitations and comprehension, and we must learn to wait on Him. Our prayers should never cease. Our trust should remain steady as we wait on Him and His perfect timing.

Yield to Him, and His glory will be visible. *Your obedience is the channel outward for the power that is at work within you.* Simply believe that He is able to do what He says. Expect Him to show up, and He will.

There is always more to life when we walk with Christ. It is a life of power and glory and the unimaginable. Are you experiencing the immeasurably more? Now is the time to begin. There is *more* to life!

About the Author

Tom and Kathy Kinnan have been married forty-eight years, and they have two married children and seven grandloves. Prior to retiring, Kathy taught humanities at Whitefield Academy, a Christian classical school, and she puts up with a weird and wacky husband.

With forty-two years of pastoring and forty-eight years of ministry, Tom brings a depth of knowledge as well as tenderness and compassion to his subject matter. Known for insight, humor, and challenging teaching, his presentations are anointed of God. Tom has traveled internationally as a speaker at colleges, churches, conventions, retreats, and camps. He has extensive experience serving missionaries and in mission fields.

Tom's heart is to see people in the church become equipped to live their lives fully devoted to Christ in the community where God plants them to be a light. He does not want to maintain a church, but wants the church to be a living and growing body of believers.

Tom is the founder and president of Good Shepherd Ministries (drtomkinnan.com) and serves with New Church Specialties as an interim pastor.

About Sermon To Book

SermonToBook.com began with a simple belief: that sermons should be touching lives, *not* collecting dust. That's why we turn sermons into high-quality books that are accessible to people all over the globe.

Turning your sermon series into a book exposes more people to God's Word, better equips you for counseling, accelerates future sermon prep, adds credibility to your ministry, and even helps make ends meet during tight times.

John 21:25 tells us that the world itself couldn't contain the books that would be written about the work of Jesus Christ. Our mission is to try anyway. Because in heaven, there will no longer be a need for sermons or books. Our time is now.

If God so leads you, we'd love to work with you on your sermon or sermon series.

Visit www.sermontobook.com to learn more.

REFERENCES

Notes

[1] *Encyclopaedia Britannica*, "charagus." https://www.britanni ca.com/art/choragus.

[2] Barclay, William. "Commentary on 2 Peter 1." *William Barclay's Daily Study Bible.* https://www.studylight.org/ commentaries/dsb/2-peter-1.html. 1956-1959.

[3] Barclay, "2 Peter 1."

[4] Bell, Daryl. Quoted in *Leadership* (Fall Quarter, 1984), p. 47 https://www.sermonsearch.com/sermon-illustrations/5635/ live-the-christian-life-little-by-little/.

[5] *Thayer's Greek Lexicon*, "Strong's G#703–ἀρέτη." https://www.studylight.org/lexicons/greek/703.html.

[6] Barclay, "2 Peter 1."

[7] Coots, Fred J., and Haven Gillespie. "Santa Clause Is Comin' to Town." Decca Records, Inc., 1934.

[8] Barclay, "2 Peter 1."

[9] Hodgin, Michael. *1001 Humorous Illustrations for Public Speaking: Fresh, Timely, and Compelling Illustrations for Preachers, Teachers, and Speakers*. Zondervan, 2010.

[10] Barclay, "2 Peter 1."

[11] Barclay, "2 Peter 1."

[12] See, for example, Bob Phillips, *The Best of the Good Clean Jokes* (Harvest House Publishers, 2013), p. 147.

[13] Kraut, Richard. "Aristotle's Ethics." *Stanford Encyclopedia of Philosophy*. 2001. https://plato.stanford.edu/entries/aristotle-ethics/#Akra.

[14] Barclay, "2 Peter 1."

[15] Barclay, "2 Peter 1."

[16] Barclay, "2 Peter 1."

[17] Barclay, "2 Peter 1."

[18] Barclay, William. *The Letters of James and Peter*. Westminster John Knox Press, 1960.

[19] Barclay, *The Letters of James and Peter*.

[20] *Blue Letter Bible*, "G26–agape." https://www.blueletterbible.org/lang/lexicon/lexicon.cfm?Strongs=G26&t=KJV.

[21] *Thayer's Greek Lexicon*, "Strong's G#2578–kámptō." https://www.studylight.org/lexicons/greek/2578.html.

[22] *Thayer's Greek Lexicon*, "Strong's G#3962–patěr." https://www.studylight.org/lexicons/greek/3962.html.

[23] Evans, Peter. *Peter Sellers: The Mask Behind the Mask*. Severn House. 1980.

[24] Lean, David. *Oliver Twist*. Cineguild, 1948.

[25] *Robertson's New Testament Word Pictures*, "NT:2901." *Biblesoft's New Exhaustive Strong's Numbers and Concordance with Expanded Greek–Hebrew Dictionary*. Biblesoft and International Bible Translators, 1994.

[26] *Thayer's Greek Lexicon*, "Strong's G#1411–dýnamis." https://www.studylight.org/lexicons/greek/1411.html.

[27] *Greek–English Lexicon* (Liddell–Scott–Jones), "Strong's G#1411–dýnamis." https://www.studylight.org/lexicons/greek/1411.html.

[28] *Thayer's Greek Lexicon*, "Strong's G#1391–dóxa." https://www.studylight.org/lexicons/greek/1391.html.

[29] "Too Tall Tidbits." *Arlington Enterprise*. March 24, 2016, p. 4. http://glencoenews.com/sites/default/files/ae3-24a1.pdf.

[30] *Blue Letter Bible*, "Strong's G2730–katoikeō." https://www.blueletterbible.org/lang/lexicon/lexicon.cfm?Strongs=G2730&t=KJV.

[31] "What's the Problem." Bible.org. https://bible.org/illustration/what's-problem.

[32] *Blue Letter Bible*, "G2729–katischyō." https://www.blueletterbible.org/lang/lexicon/lexicon.cfm?Strongs=G2729&t=KJV.

[33] *Blue Letter Bible*, "G1840–exischyō." https://www.blueletterbible.org/lang/lexicon/lexicon.cfm?Strongs=G1840&t=KJV.

[34] *Blue Letter Bible*, "G2480–ischyō." https://www.blueletterbible.org/lang/lexicon/lexicon.cfm?strongs=G2480&t=K

JV.

[35] *Robertson's New Testament Word Pictures*, "NT:1840." *Biblesoft's New Exhaustive Strong's Numbers and Concordance with Expanded Greek–Hebrew Dictionary.* Biblesoft and International Bible Translators, 1994.

[36] *Vine's Expository Dictionary of NT Words*, "apprehend." https://www.studylight.org/dictionaries/eng/ved/a/apprehend. html.

[37] White, T. H. *The Book of Merlyn: The Conclusion to* The Once and Future King. University of Texas Press, 2018.

[38] Vine, William Edwy, Unger, Merrill Fredrick, and White, William. *Vine's Expository Dictionary of Biblical Words.* Thomas Nelson Publishers, 1985.

[39] Olsen, Irene Francis. "Lee Iacocca." Living: The Ultimate Team Sport. https://babyboomersandmore.com/tag/lee-iacocca/.

[40] *Thayer's Greek Lexicon*, "Strong's #4137–plēróō." https://www.studylight.org/lexicons/greek/4137.html.

[41] *Thayer's Greek Lexicon*, "Strong's #4138–plērōma." https://www.studylight.org/lexicons/greek/4138.html.

[42] "Too Tall Tidbits," *Arlington Enterprise.*

[43] *Thayer's Greek Lexicon*, "Strongs #1410–dýnamai." https://www.studylight.org/lexicons/greek/1410.html.

[44] Lucado, Max. *No Wonder They Call Him the Savior.* Thomas Nelson, Inc., 2009.

[45] Thompson, Rick. "G. Campbell Morgan." Bible.org. 2009. https://bible.org/node/14043.

[46] Tanner, Clark. "To God Be the Glory." Sermoncentral.com. 2003. https://www.sermoncentral.com/sermons/to-god-be-the-glory-clark-tanner-sermon-on-gods-omnipotence-56309?page=4.

96805736R00105